The Nolympics

NICHOLAS LEZARD

The Nolympics
*One Man's Struggle Against
Sporting Hysteria*

With illustrations by David Shrigley

PENGUIN BOOKS

PENGUIN BOOKS

Published by the Penguin Group
Penguin Books Ltd, 80 Strand, London WC2R ORL, England
Penguin Group (USA) Inc., 375 Hudson Street, New York, New York 10014, USA
Penguin Group (Canada), 90 Eglinton Avenue East, Suite 700, Toronto, Ontario, Canada
M4P 2Y3 (a division of Pearson Penguin Canada Inc.)
Penguin Ireland, 25 St Stephen's Green, Dublin 2, Ireland (a division of Penguin Books Ltd)
Penguin Group (Australia), 707 Collins Street, Melbourne, Victoria 3008, Australia
(a division of Pearson Australia Group Pty Ltd)
Penguin Books India Pvt Ltd, 11 Community Centre, Panchsheel Park, New Delhi – 110 017, India
Penguin Group (NZ), 67 Apollo Drive, Rosedale, Auckland 0632, New Zealand
(a division of Pearson New Zealand Ltd)
Penguin Books (South Africa) (Pty) Ltd, Block D, Rosebank Office Park,
181 Jan Smuts Avenue, Parktown North, Gauteng 2193, South Africa

Penguin Books Ltd, Registered Offices: 80 Strand, London WC2R ORL, England

www.penguin.com

First published 2012
001

Copyright © Nicholas Lezard, 2012
Illustrations copyright © David Shrigley, 2012
All rights reserved

The moral right of the author has been asserted

Set in 10.5/14pt Sabon LT std
Typeset by Jouve (UK), Milton Keynes
Printed in England by Clays Ltd, St Ives plc

ISBN: 978-0-718-19761-2

www.greenpenguin.co.uk

ALWAYS LEARNING   **PEARSON**

For my parents

Even as a runner who stops in the heat of the
race, trying to understand the meaning of it all:
to meditate is an admission that one is winded.

E. M. Cioran, *Anathemas and Admirations*

Introduction

First, we have to go back to the year 50 BC.

In a clearing in a wood in the northwestern corner of ancient Gaul, a Roman athlete is training for the Olympic Games. He runs past two flummoxed Gaulish warriors – a big fat one, and a small, wiry one – who are in the woods to hunt boar. 'What's the matter with that Roman?' asks the bigger warrior. 'I haven't a clue,' replies the smaller one. 'Perhaps someone's after him.' So the fat warrior runs after the athlete, his legs moving so fast that they are no more individually discernible than the spinning blades of an aeroplane's propellor. Holding on to his helmet to stop it from falling off with his velocity, he courteously asks the Roman if anyone is after him. Then the little warrior, his own legs moving as fast as his companion's, comes up on the other side – to the astonishment of the Roman – and says, 'Leave that Roman alone, and let's go and find some boars.' 'All right,' he agrees, and off they zoom away from the Olympian. 'They overtook me!' he says, crushed. 'Both of them!'

He recovers his self-confidence and, uprooting a sapling slightly taller than himself, says: 'Anyway, when it comes to throwing the javelin ... I'm the greatest!' (This last, we know, has been his watchword – up until now, as it turns out.) He hurls the sapling into the woods. But, as he shades his eyes and looks into the distance, back comes a massive tree-trunk, which hits him – PAAAF! – right in the face.

These are the first humiliations experienced by the legionary Gluteus Maximus, a character in Goscinny and Uderzo's *Asterix at the Olympic Games*. First published in French in 1968, to coincide with the Games of Mexico City, and then in English translation (by Anthea Bell and Derek Hockridge) in 1972, to coincide with the Munich Games, this work remains, nearly half a century later, as fresh and useful a guide to the ideals (and potential corruption of those ideals) of the Olympics as anything you will find (or at least that can also be understood by the average ten-year-old). For those who do not know, the reason the Gauls in these woods can run so fast is because their druid, Getafix,* brews a magic potion which gives all who drink it superhuman strength. Thus they are able to repel the invaders; the last village in Gaul to do so. When they hear about the Olympic Games – once they find out what Gluteus Maximus (a big, blond, Aryan brute of a man) has been up to in the woods – they decide they want to take part, too. They are stymied when told that they cannot, as only Hellenes and, by special dispensation, Romans, are allowed to. But then Asterix has a brainwave: 'But, by Toutatis . . . we ARE Romans!' 'Since

---

* The name in French is the neutral, unfunny Panoramix. The English name, coined by a mischievous Bell at the height of druggy hippydom, would not now be allowed. That it passed by The Man in the first place was only because, back in those days, English publishing was not the refuge for the hip and the streetwise that it is now.

when?' 'Since old Julius conquered Gaul! He's commented on the subject at length, hasn't he?'*

And so begins a very funny story with all the elements familiar to a modern audience: the dodgy adoption of nationality, crowd partisanship, the thirst for victory and the political capital that comes with it, sporting hysteria, overconfidence, lack of discipline in the Olympic Village and – above all – doping. In the book's *dénouement* (I would advise those of you who would rather discover this for yourselves to skip to the next paragraph) the Romans, who have been lured to a cauldron of the potion by the cunning Asterix and Getafix, are revealed as cheats. Getafix has added a 'permitted colouring matter' to the potion, and all those who have drunk of it have had their tongues turned blue. We discover what the Romans' tongues look like when Asterix accuses them by sticking his own tongue out and shouting, 'Cheats! YAAAH!' The Romans, *en masse*, unwisely reply with the same gesture, 'YAAAH yourself!'

You might not think this worth mentioning had not various commentators been baffled by the appearance, usually post-victory, of athletes prominently sporting blue tongues. The BBC website had this to say about it:

A number of readers noticed that Team GB football goalkeeper Jack Butland and a number of other athletes appeared

---

* Julius Caesar, *Commentarii de Bello Gallico*, eight vols., check your local bookstore or, if you must, online retailer for purchase details. (The work actually appeared posthumously, but Asterix is allowed his joke here, I think.)

to have unusually blue tongues. No definitive answer can be given, but the culprit might appear to be a blue drink provided by sponsor Powerade.

Even Powerade says it isn't certain, but adds: 'The berry and tropical flavour does have the potential to temporarily colour tongues in berry-like shades.'

Now, I am not at all saying that the real reason these athletes had blue tongues was because they overheard that, in the shed over there with the door that doesn't shut properly, the one that isn't guarded at night, there was a cauldron of magic potion laced with permitted colouring matter. I'm just mentioning the coincidence, that's all.

My own experience of the Olympics is confined to 1972, the first and, really, the last time I caught anything like Olympic fever.

It was the year of Mark Spitz and Olga Korbut, whose too-young body nevertheless inspired strange yearnings in me (I was nine; does that make it better, or worse?), and it represented the high-water mark of my interest in athletic events. When you're nine you lap up all sorts of easily digested rubbish. Reading about earlier London Games in 1908 and 1948 in my copies of *World of Wonder*, and happy to buy into and endorse a sense of blind patriotic entitlement, I spent some years wishing badly that they would return here. This was a real, deeply felt wish. And then the fever died away, I started thinking of other things, and, without a regret, put my Olympian feelings in the recycling bin, where they mulched into hopes for a country that would be at ease with itself, proud and with good conscience, where one could be safe and happy in the knowledge that one's taxes were going to maintain hospitals, pensions, the relief of poverty, and not pay for the bonuses of bankers or for the meaningless achievements of those who might have a chance of running around an elliptical track faster than anyone else, for all the good that would do anyone but themselves.

I assure you, though, that this never stopped me from wanting us to thrash Australia again one day at cricket. There are some feelings that never die.

And this year was proving very trying: there had been an overdose of Union flags leading to a kind of pattern blindness; the wedding between William Windsor and Katherine Middleton had left me utterly unmoved. I have form on being unmoved by royal weddings. When I was younger, the prospect of the nuptials of Charles and Diana had propelled me out of the country. Eighteen years old, I holed up, thanks to tenuous, and since broken, family connections, in an attic room in a smart part of Paris; seven floors up, in what the French call a *chambre de bonne*, a maid's room, with the only private bathroom facility a sink barely large enough to wash my balls. My French landlords resided in splendour four floors below, where they graciously invited me to a small party whose central attraction would be the broadcast of the wedding service. I had arrived in France a month or so after the Brixton riots; the shock was still raw, and my sympathies were – and remain – with the rioters rather than the police. To celebrate a union ensuring the continuation of a system that perpetuated the kind of social divisions that would make such violent demonstrations not only inevitable but excusable seemed to me obscene. (Not that I had anything against Diana, who, a helpless product of her upbringing, still did more to undermine the principle of monarchy than any republican. Moved, much moved in fact, to my astonishment, by her death, in that crazy summer of 1997, with the landslide election of an as-yet-untainted Labour government, when the country collectively lost its mind in both grief and excitement, I learned that I was not, after all, immune to the feelings of my fellow-citizens* and that not all mass

---

* For the record, I am a dual national: British and American, with an American mother and an English father. This is not entirely irrelevant. My mother, the child of Polish immigrants, brought up in the insecurity of poverty and in her time a fundraiser for those of her showbusiness colleagues who had been persecuted by McCarthy and the House of Unamerican Activities, would always make fun of the Queen's hats, by extension mocking the monarchy and the class system of this country. Moreover, she would glance at the football being shown on television and say, scornfully, 'Oh look, the man put the ball in the net.' Or, of cricket, 'Oh look, the man hit the ball with the stick.' My father, on the other hand, was a product of Stowe School (a private establishment that tends to favour its cricket players over its academics, although George Melly went there, and famously seduced Peregrine Worsthorne while a pupil). He played cricket for the Old Stoics, Trinity, Cambridge, and MCC, and was a natural sportsman: a man who could probably have picked up a pelota bat and been in the running for the Basque team after a day or two's practice. At one stage it looked as though I was destined for Stowe too, until my mother put her foot down; its reputation appeared to have crossed the Atlantic, even into the dives of Philadelphia and Atlantic City.

My parents' marriage has, with glorious improbability, survived, but I am the product of a pro- and anti-sport union. I understand the arguments in favour of it, and against it, in theory at least; in practice, my habits tend towards complete physical indolence, and it is a testament to

popular movements are ignoble, unworthy or the first step on the road to consensual tyranny.)

The Toxteth riots came afterwards. My French landlords called me down to see those, too, and I thought, now that's more like it, but my instincts are against any mass popular movement which involves flag-waving. I also remember being frightened and horrified by the surge of jingoism that put the wind in the sails of the fleet which sailed towards the Falklands in 1982, for all that I loathed the Galtieri regime of Argentina and accepted the justice, however barmy it seemed to me, of the islanders' wish to remain British. As far as I'm concerned, the only flag that gives me the creeps more than the Union Jack is the cross of St George, because at least the Jack testifies to a union of countries, whereas the plain red on white motif indicates you can't even bear the thought of being allied to Scotland or the other ones.

As for my interest in sports . . . well, this isn't going to keep us long. In athletics, I considered it a triumph if I didn't come last in a race. This is not an exaggeration. Boxing? Don't make me laugh. There was a brief window between my finding that I enjoyed diving off a high board – conquering terror is not only hugely rewarding to the self, it's free – and my eyesight getting so bad that I couldn't see the surface of the water I was hurtling towards. Tennis I actually liked, but I gave that up when my sixty-something mother-in-law beat me on a court in Harpenden. Darts I respect; snooker I

---

the seriousness with which I have treated the writing of this small book that I have mostly done so sitting at a desk, as opposed to, as is my usual habit when I write, in bed.

love, but my best break is in the very, very low twenties, and probably always will be. Football, to play, disgusts me – if football had a consciousness I think I would be able to say that the feeling was mutual – but I love it to bits by comparison with what I think about rugby.

On sports day every year, when I was between the ages of eight and thirteen, a teacher would place something bizarre, such as a discus or a javelin, in my bewildered hands and I would try to fling it as far away from me as I could, but pretty much everyone else could fling it further. Cricket remains the only game I can both play and watch till the cows come home. At the more rural grounds, this is more than just a turn of phrase. I think we're done now; you get the idea.

So: combine athletic sport and flag-waving, and you have pretty much the two things that I dislike most about the modern and ancient worlds, short of slavery, genocide and boy bands. When my friend Zoe, a woman wiser than her years and with a gift for the invective phrase, announced her intention to avoid every second of the Olympics, and added, before it started, 'It's all ball bags,' I was in no mood to contradict her.

Then, of course, there was the run-up to the Games. I have a document, thirteen pages long and consisting almost entirely of URLs, in which I noted every cock-up that announced itself in the months leading to the Big Day. It is a diary of dyspepsia, which it would be wearisome for me to reprint and you to read, so – pausing only to mention its first item: the story that residents of Newham were advised not to die during the Games as funeral cortèges would be impossibly delayed – instead, I give you a brief piece I wrote for the *Big Issue*, published on the day before the Games started, which neatly summarizes my feelings at the time, and also goes to show just how wrong you can be.

Let us start with the silliest thing of all. We all know examples of this kind of thing – but here, at the time of writing, is just the latest: a café in Camberwell, which put up, in its front window, five bagels arranged in the familiar pattern of the Olympic logo, has been ordered to take them down. Well, you might say, this café is actually on the Olympic Torch route, so its proprietor might have been asking for trouble – and, to be fair to the Olympic brand police, it was actually wardens from Southwark Borough Council who jumped the gun and told him off. The marvel is that any human being who considers him- or herself a free agent could decide to interpret the law in such a fashion on their own initiative.

And it is also possible that this may be the last such instance of this insanity. The government has finally worked out that such heavy-handedness is tainting what doubtless some people somewhere are calling 'the whole Olympic brand' and is trying to let small businesses off the hook when it comes to the zealous application of the rules, but we shall have to wait and see how much wiggle room the Olympic Games and Paralympic Games Act of 2006 allows them, or how much the International Olympic Committee are prepared to give them – or how much the sponsors themselves will.

The big joke, or the not-so-funny side to this all, depending on how you look at it, comes when you compare the zeal and efficiency with which grannies baking cakes, or knitting dolls, or arranging floral displays with Olympic rings on them hundreds of miles away from the Games have been prosecuted, and the staggering ineptitude which has characterized G4S's possibly more important job of providing anything like the number of competent, trained security officers needed in order to ensure that a terrorist outrage does not happen in a crowded Olympic venue. (As it is, we have since learned that such security staff as we have are being trained to sniff out the difference between water and vodka, and not between water and, say, liquid trinitrotoluene.)

It has come to this because it was always going to be like this. I would argue that this is the way power trends: it's the direction it pursues, and once you have abandoned – or bought off – the constraints, this kind of thing is inevitable. At the moment it may make for some medium-level indignation of the kind that sees, most unusually, both bolshie grumblers like me and the *Daily Mail* singing from the same hymn sheet for once, but unless some kind of reaction kicks in, or we wake up to the direction we're heading, and the way the world could turn out, we are going to be living in the kind of nightmare that not even George Orwell could have imagined. His 1984 was a grey place, a monoculture where you could only drink one beer, or smoke one kind of cigarette, where every brand of everything was called 'Victory'. But suddenly we wake to find ourselves – especially if we are within 100 metres of an Olympic venue – in a garishly coloured monoculture, where we are only allowed to drink one kind of beer, one soft drink, and eat one kind of food.

You may say that it's a good thing that at least there isn't an Official Olympic Cigarette; but it isn't exactly as if Coke and Heineken and McDonald's feature very much in the diets of the world's top performing athletes, either.

Let us consider this: that there is a connection between the so-called Olympic Ideal and the will to power. I was going to say 'predatory capitalism' but this goes beyond the whole left/right debate. The official Olympic Ideal, I was surprised to learn, goes like this: 'the premise that individuals, not countries, compete against each other in sport . . . [in] peaceful competition without the burden of politics, religion, or racism.' As far as this goes, it looks OK, but last time we checked, the medals tables have little flags next to them, not little pictures of the individuals who have won them.

The problem lies in the confusion between countries and individuals. Ever since we saw Soviets and East Germans with the physiques of stevedores and the flourishing moustaches of Victorian circus ringmasters competing in the women's weightlifting and shot-putt events, we have known that a rough indication of how depraved a country is can be seen in how far it is prepared to go, how far it is prepared to interfere with the natural processes of humanity, in order to sit more comfortably at the top of the medals table. This is, look at it any way you like, at the very least, an immature way of going about things. It is, for one thing, childish, and for another, it fools, or should fool, no one. But still they do it: the despots looked at the way the founders of the regenerated games equated moral worth with athletic success, and decided that that was the way forward, or one of them.

This is the *übermensch* mentality that, of course, the Nazis rammed down the world's throats in the 1936 Games – where, incidentally, the idea of running the torch from Athens to the host city was dreamed up. No one looking at those Games was left in any doubt afterwards that that was what the Nazis wanted the world to look like, just in the way the chairmen of Coke, Heineken and McDonald's dream of a whole world where no one else is allowed to sell any competing product. And is it a coincidence or not, I wonder, that the architect responsible for the design of the 2008 Beijing Olympics was the son and, indeed, the namesake, of Hitler's own favourite architect, Albert Speer?

NOTE TO THE READER

You are reading this at leisure; it has been written, and then edited, in frantic haste. This has been the whole point of the exercise. So if not forgive, then at least understand, such mistakes of fact, punctuation, sentence structure, amnesiac repetition or other weird glitches that have escaped the vigilance of writer or editor. Errors of opinion – if you can have such a thing – and interpretation – a thing you certainly can have – are the author's own responsibility entirely.

27 July 2012

DAY 0

....

The Hysteria Begins
The Opening Ceremony

....

The day of the opening ceremony dawns. The fine weather of the last few days has reverted to this summer's endless rain. An email from a fellow-sceptic alerts me to Boris Johnson 'blustering on Radio 4'. Never mind: I don't *have* to listen to him (although duty will probably oblige me to catch up on this jackanapes later on in the day). Big Ben has been given dispensation to chime for three full minutes at 8.12 a.m. (This is a Cultural Olympiad thing, the idea being that everyone should ring a bell as loudly as possible for three minutes at this time. Culture Secretary Jeremy Hunt nearly brains a woman as the handle of his bell breaks, inaugurating a swiftly spreading rash of jokes about 'bell-ends'. The art thing is presumably a nod towards 8.12 p.m., i.e. 20:12, by which time people will be too excited by the run-up to the opening ceremony to do anything artistic.) Although I am not in the vicinity at the time, I am worried, for the disruption of its normal ringing pattern is traditionally reserved for much better reasons, such as, in *Thunderball*, the agreed signal by the government that it will accept the terms of nuclear extortion by SPECTRE.

On the *Today* programme on Radio 4, no one seems to be mentioning anything that is not directly concerned with the Games. John Major, the prime minister who, to his own lasting regret, though that is not alluded to this morning, sold off more school playing fields than any other, is unctuously praising the spectacle in advance. An unforeseen horror: the rifling through the dripping bins of history to dig out whoever they can to give the Games a cheer. The programme ends with a five-minute-long sound montage of hysterical commentary recorded from previous Olympics, the voices distorted by both mania and distance. The clips have been chosen to represent British victories over the years, so at least they do not have *too* many to choose from. All the same, the relentless barrage is unbearable, and only disbelief – *how* long are they going to keep this up for? – and a grim sense of duty keep me from snapping the radio off. 'No! No! Unbelievable!' 'He's got to dig deep! He's got to go somewhere really dark!' 'I don't care what you're doing! If you're not standing, get up on your feet!' It is as if Alan Partridge had never been created. In fact, compared to these freakishly excited commentators, Partridge sounds like John Snagge, or any one of those staid, unflappable relics from pre-war days, who read the news in evening dress and are now mocked by Harry Enfield, who knows better.

So: I had worried, if that is the word, that I too might have been swept up in the general celebrations. After listening to the radio for about ten minutes, I suspect that this is not going to be the case. I have a nasty feeling that exposure to any media other than a book will mean having to endure, in effect, someone screaming the word 'Olympics!' at me without a break for the next seventeen days. You can't even escape it on Radio 3: they have a composer on before 9 a.m. who has written some music 'for the torch'.

Earlier, John Major had pointed out that the National Lottery resulted in a huge increase in our medal haul. I have to admit he has a point. Here are the figures for the last twenty years. In Barcelona 1992: 376 competitors, 20 medals, came 13th; Atlanta 1996: 300, 15, came 36th; Sydney 2000: 332, 28, 10th; Athens 2004: 259, 31, 10th; Beijing 2008: 312, 47, 4th (beating Germany; behind China, US and Russia).

All jolly good, of course, and that leap to fourth place is quite impressive (although, historically, Team GB – as it wasn't called in happier days – comes third overall in terms of gold medals won), but it would have been perhaps more worthwhile if the funds which helped towards such improvement had been used to, say, keep libraries or hospitals open, or train a few teachers. Does one imagine that the citizens of Russia or China feel significantly less immiserated, or freer, because of their strong showing in the medals tables in recent years? How is Greece doing these days, after having enjoyed its home advantage in 2004 with its respectable haul of six golds (fifteenth place)? Certainly it gives a population, and a government, something easy to point at, a kind of index of superiority that would be comprehensible to a caveman; indices of happiness, or freedom, or cultural and intellectual robustness might be harder to quantify (and, in the instances of many of the countries represented, undesirable in the first place).

Beyond this there is, of course, the so-called 'Cultural Olympiad', which has been taking place in the months preceding the Games, in which various pieces which may be loosely categorized as performance art have been put on throughout the country. I have chosen not to write about them for two reasons: the first is that the Olympiad's director, Ruth Mackenzie, is an old friend of mine, and so I fear that any criticisms I might have to make about it would be compromised; and the second is that as far as I have been able to gather, the Olympiad, like a poetry slam, has made little impression on anyone apart from those intimately involved in its execution and those obliged to see the performances in person (with, very often, an enormous overlap between the two groups).

Talking of armies: I see my first Olympic-branded soldiers, the last-minute replacements for the security that the mesmerizingly incompetent G4S failed to provide, despite some advance notice, on the streets: a small squad of squaddies at ease – very much at ease – outside the Sue Ryder charity shop in Crawford Street. Their London 2012 patches stand out on their camouflaged arms like garish boy scout badges, the kind that are awarded for nothing much except simply turning up somewhere on time. They seem to be unarmed, which pleases me, and wordlessly ogle a group of three lunch-breaking women. They are not exceptionally beautiful, but we should bear in mind that, if the soldiers have just come back from Afghanistan, these are the first women's knees they have seen, with impunity, for months.

I nip out to the bookshop to replace my lost copy of Janie Hampton's *The Austerity Olympics*, an account of the 1948 London Games, pick up, with more than the anticipated disgust, the *London 2012 Olympic Games: The Official Book* with a foreword by Sebastian Coe KBE, and a copy of *Jeeves in the Offing*, which I will turn to for solace and balm when it all Gets Too Much, and intend to read, with a torch, under the duvet, where no one can get me. The last page of the official book has a photo of the medals for the Olympics: unsurprisingly, they are emblazoned with the disgusting logo, and criss-crossed with raised welts of more or less random-seeming distribution, as if after an attack by a crazed fencer. The Chinese medals from 2008, by comparison, are things of austere beauty. However revolting their government is, they at least had the sense to get a decent designer for their baubles. Their torch was loads nicer, too.

Then, suddenly, I get a most unexpected inkling as to how my, and other sceptics', attitude is not as entrenched as it might be: Mitt Romney, on the British leg of a world tour (and stopping off en route to attend a $75,000 a head fundraising dinner at the Royal Mandarin Hotel, the tickets being sold, mainly, to hedge-fund investors and people of similarly questionable popularity and integrity), has suggested that London might not be ready for the Games. He cites the proposed strike by border officials, the G4S cockup, and misgivings among the general populace – in fact, pretty much exactly some of the things I have been grumbling about. Yet, for reasons which do not need too much examination, I – and not only I, but pretty much everyone in the country who hears about this – take exception to the remarks of this overprivileged idiot (whose wife, incidentally, has a horse competing in the dressage, or, as I suddenly decide to call it, horsey dancing. Romney is not keen to associate himself with this involvement, it seems). We reserve the right to complain for ourselves, in the way that we will ferociously rally to the defence of a family member, long despaired of, when maligned by an outsider. Boris Johnson, addressing a rally of some 60,000 people in Hyde Park, says 'there's this guy called Mitt Romney who says we aren't ready. Are we ready?' The crowd roars back that we are, and then – and this is quite an extraordinary moment, I must say, and a prime example of Johnson's ability to outflank his enemies, among whom I number myself – gets everyone to chant Barack Obama's slogan 'Yes we can' several times. This would be insulting enough to Romney even if Johnson were not, notionally, a political ally of Romney's.

So, as we settle down in front of the telly, a couple of things are worth recording. Amir Khan says we have to be 'calm and collective'. And Andrew Marr makes, as if he were the first person to make it, the exhausted point about London being a global village (the first time London must have been described as a 'global village' was in 43 BC, when it was, actually, a village), ready to welcome anyone with open arms. I recall the flurry that happened when it was announced, barely two weeks beforehand, that David Cameron had been making noises recently about banning, specifically, Greeks, from coming to the United Kingdom.

Then there was the ceremony. I think almost everything that it has been necessary to say about the opening ceremony has been said. But not everything. The first is that it makes best sense as a dream, and, as is the case with dreams, what has not been said, but only alluded to, being as important as what is. So although the snatch, very near the beginning, of the Sex Pistols' 'God Save the Queen' does not include its next line, 'the fascist regime', we hear it anyway. And when Kenneth Branagh, dressed as Brunel, declaims the 'isle is full of noises' speech, those who know their Shakespeare will know that after Caliban says 'when I waked/I cried to dream again', the context is that he is getting terribly excited at throwing off the suzerainty of Prospero. Immediately afterwards, Stefano says, 'this will prove a brave kingdom to me, where I shall have my music for nothing' (strangely contemporary, that), and Caliban replies, 'when Prospero is destroyed'. For Caliban is native to the island; Prospero an invader.

And here is the other thing: commentators said, and for days and days thereafter *ad nauseam* said, what a good sport the Queen was when allowing herself to look as though she was parachuting into the stadium with the current James Bond, even going so far as to say – according to Boris Johnson, whose testimony may be legitimately regarded as partial and possibly a stretching of the truth (he has form on this, after all) – that it was 'a bit of a laugh' (not her style of speech, one would think). Every commentator said that this was a refreshing example of that hitherto under-represented phenomenon, the Royal Sense of Humour, but I saw her expression throughout the ceremony: her mouth grimly unsmiling (she can smile without self-consciousness, but usually when a horse of hers is doing well), and, at least at one point, even looking down at her lap, as if she were texting someone. She wasn't, by any of the conventional readings of human expression, enjoying herself, and a far more plausible interpretation of her mien was that she was bubbling with fury at the outrageous and humiliating *lèse majesté* that had been visited on her royal person, her acquiescence in this stunt explicable only by the sense of obligation that is one of her better characteristics, occasioned in this instance by the realization that this was payback for all the uncritical sycophancy over her Diamond Jubilee earlier in the year. One marvels not only at Danny Boyle's cheek in managing even to propose this sequence, but also at the government's decision not to veto it. I heard it, from very good authority, that just a week before the ceremony an anxious Culture Secretary, the unfortunate Jeremy Hunt, had told Boyle that the show was 'not Tory enough', and had begged for the NHS celebration to be removed. We will probably only fully discover what went on at this meeting under the thirty-year rule, in 2042 – if then.

As I read *The Austerity Olympics*, I am staggered to come across the words of 'Non Nobis, Domine', a Kipling poem set in 1934 for choir by Roger Quilter. There are three verses; the song was sung in its entirety at the opening ceremony of 1948. Here is the second verse.

> And we confess our blame,
> How all too high we hold
> That noise which men call Fame,
> That dross which men call Gold.

For these we undergo
Our hot and godless days,
But in our hearts we know
Not unto us the Praise.

In other news: Syrian tanks roll towards Aleppo, preparing
to massacre their own citizens.

28 July 2012

DAY 1

....

Splatalot
Rowing
Women's 10m Air Rifle
Cycling
Dressage

....

The party atmosphere after the opening ceremony is too intense to allow me to sleep, and I do not, in the end, go to bed until dawn starts to break. I have been thoroughly discomfited, wrong-footed. Still, it is pleasing to discover that I have not been cauterized within, that there is a part of me which actually is capable of engaging with a crowd and with entertainments for crowds. Later on, I am alerted to a *Daily Mail* article – which is subsequently, following a couple of days of combined protest and ridicule, first substantially re-edited, and then taken down completely – by one Rick Dewsbury, whose headline runs 'The NHS did not deserve to be so disgracefully glorified in this bonanza of left-wing propaganda', and which contains the following amazing sentences:

But it was the absurdly unrealistic scene – and indeed one that would spring from the kind of nonsensical targets and equality quotas we see in the NHS – showing a mixed-race middle-class family in a detached new-build suburban home, which was most symptomatic of the politically correct agenda in modern Britain.

This was supposed to be a representation of modern life in England but it is likely to be a challenge for the organizers to find an educated white middle-aged mother and black father living together with a happy family in such a set-up.

Almost, if not every, shot in the next sequence included an ethnic minority performer. The BBC presenter Hazel Irvine gushed about the importance of grime music (a form of awful electronic music popular among black youths) to east London. This multicultural equality agenda was so staged it was painful to watch.

So my delight at the ceremony, all the more poignant for being radically unanticipated, is consolidated – not that it needed much consolidation.

On rising at around 10.30 the next morning, I am tired. When I turn on the telly I see a group of children with helmets being squirted with foam fired from a water cannon by a charismatically insolent bearded man wearing goggles. At one point, as if to illustrate his insouciance, he pours some of the foam into a silver teacup and sips from it with provocative delicacy. What new Olympic sport is this? I know that there is a drive towards populism, but even so this does seem rather . . . *niche*. It certainly makes beach volleyball look positively Corinthian. It gradually dawns on me that I have tuned to BBC2 by mistake and am watching a children's programme called *Splatalot*. I expect to see it as a fully accepted international sport some time around the XXXIVth Olympiad of the modern era.

I switch back to BBC1 and see Great Britain, Argentina, New Zealand and Estonia competing in the two-man sculls. (With the British flag prominently displayed at the start, I begin once more to feel that sense of Union Jack overload, the same pattern blindness that overwhelmed me during the Jubilee festivities earlier.) They are rowing past grass-lined banks, their crafts nudging ahead a little faster with each stroke, then flowing back as the water drags against the hulls. A few cyclists lazily follow them along the towpath. It looks rather pleasant, bucolic. But the problem with rowing, *qua* spectator sport, is that once the boats have been set in motion, the result is apparent long before it is over, barring some superhuman effort or disaster. Years of watching the Oxford/Cambridge Boat Race have taught me this; and that the sport, on that occasion at least, is really not much more than an excuse for a piss-up. But it is too early for that, so I go to breakfast. And on the way I contemplate the opening ceremony, and find – perhaps this is one of those hangovers where one feels particularly emotionally labile, perhaps not – my eyes pricking with tears.

The theme of the green and pleasant land is maintained by the cycling, in the early afternoon, as the riders whizz through Dorking, up and down Box Hill, a route familiar to me from my childhood. Cycling is one of those sports that has evolved from what one imagines must have been rather straightforward origins into something more arcane and perplexing. I have had it explained to me more than once what a *péloton* is, but never has an explanation stuck, or succeeded in overcoming my irreducible conviction of what one would have thought was the point of a race: to start it, and have the fastest competitor win it. (Apparently it has something to do with overcoming wind resistance, but this is not a book of sporting explanations.)

Anyway, there is a moment comprehensible to a three-year-old when a rider crashes into a bank of spectators, or rather the fencing in front of them, and later on we see that remarkable spectacle, suggestive of a sport whose participants will do anything to win (it is, allegedly, the most doped-up sport in the world, and its earliest competitors were pioneers of stimulant drugs; given the demands of the sport, one has more than a faint sympathy for such tactics), of a rider being treated for his injuries, while riding his bike, from a moving car.

The accident has caused a swift revision of plan among his team-mates, apparently; they had meant to do that thing which means they don't win but the number one does; now they cannot hang back and wait, for then all will be lost, but simply forge ahead and try and win themselves, as God originally intended bicycle races to be run, I think. The ride from Dorking to Knightsbridge seems to go by incredibly quickly, far faster than my father ever managed it in a car during my childhood trips to Auntie Avis, and by no means because the coverage is so exciting that the minutes are flying by like seconds, but because, I suppose (a) the roads are clear and (b) they're going like the clappers.

Not having any real interest in who actually wins this race, I look up from my notes to find that it is over, and someone has; but I hope you will forgive me if I fail to mention his name. This is not a book of results, after all. A post-match interview with a selection of cyclists makes me alert to something that I suspect I will become aware of increasingly as the games progress: that they all look the same. Not identical: you might, if knocked over by one in a hurry, have trouble identifying the culprit in a police line-up, but if you were seated round a dinner table you would, after proper introductions and with maybe some kind of mnemonic as recommended to those who are bad at remembering names, be able to identify each one separately by the time the cheese came round. But there is certainly a *type*: a kind of laterally flattened head, like a sculpture by Giacometti, a long, thin nose, and slightly protuberant eyes. But in the repose of the interview room, they all seem to have nice smiles. (And do not give any clear indication that they deserve the opprobrium suggested by my colleague Mr Shrigley's drawing of one of them. Perhaps he, once, was run over by a competitive cyclist.)

There is a little bit of dressage. Once again, and I fear this will become a refrain all too familiar throughout this little book, here is a sport whose rules, let alone intricacies, I have, despite nearly half a century on the planet, utterly failed to grasp. There are no jumps, for a start, but although I understand the difference between the flat season and the other one in horse-racing, speed is not, I gather, primarily of the essence in dressage.

But there is something mildly compelling about the spectacle, although I acknowledge that this may largely be a function of my own perverted appreciation of the women's dressage uniform. I am not alone in this; the comedian Steve Coogan afflicted his immortal creation, Alan Partridge, with an identical peccadillo, which is, after all, conventional enough.

This certainly helped me through what would otherwise have been unmitigated *longueurs* in trying to work out why one kind of prancing by the horse is rewarded by the judges, while another kind of prancing is penalized. Childhood memories of the Horse of the Year Show do not help, and all that I dredge up is the theme tune, Mozart's *Ein Musikalischer Spaß* (A Musical Joke), and the useless realization that maybe it was childhood exposure to the programme that sowed the seeds of my impractical fetish. Also, in Horse of the Year, the jumps were made out of blocks, as if they were so much gigantic Lego, and even the dimmest viewer could work out that the more of them a horse knocked down, the less likely it was going to be to win. (I also have affectionate memories of the Yorkshire and GB rider Harvey Smith, whose name became a synonym for the V-sign, after a splendid use of the gesture at the 1971 British Show Jumping Derby, which made the whole nation love a Yorkshireman for the first time.)

Two women are shown riding before the BBC moves on: Nicola Wilson, 'a lovely Yorkshire girl', and Mary King, an equally spirited woman, but, at fifty-one, rather older. She rides a horse called Imperial Cavalier, which would, if one did not know this already, suggest to the intelligent but uninformed spectator that this is not a sport at which a kid from a problem family living in an inner-city estate is going to thrive. Mary King looks exactly like Nicola Wilson, only older, and they both look exactly like the Queen's niece, Zara Phillips, who will be competing tomorrow. That Zara Phillips is both absurdly well-connected and yet also good at her sport does not bother me in the slightest; indeed it is pleasing to find a member of the royal family actually more than competent at something.

Before all this, I caught the women's 10m air rifle event. I have to salute the Olympics: this is perhaps the most awesomely uninvolving sport that a spectator could hope to see. This is not because I disdain the sport: on the contrary, it is one of the relatively few I know anything about. I, too, have an air rifle (swiped from my father once I had determined beyond doubt that his eyesight was no longer good enough to use it), and even the two types of .22 pellet that go with it: the pointy ones for shooting rats, and the flat-headed ones for target shooting. (Counterintuitively, air currents can make the pointy ones deviate from a straight trajectory more than they can the flat-headed ones, which just barrel on ahead regardless.) But my father's wartime Webley, a timelessly sleek confection of wood and steel, looks nothing like the contraptions used in modern shooting, which bring to mind either, depending on one's distracted mood, the exposed internal scaffolding of the Terminator, or the bespoke rifle commissioned by the Jackal to assassinate de Gaulle, constructed so as to be able to fit into the hollow aluminium tubes of a crutch to evade detection. Only the sport is not as exciting as that: there is a 'pft' noise, and the small distance to target means that the shooter, if she is any good, is basically putting a pellet through the hole made by the previous shot. But the competition is wrapped up early, the Chinese Yi wins the first gold of the tournament, and all the women air rifle shooters can pack up their rifles, or unscrew them, or whatever they do with these hi-tech pieces of kit, abandon their coaches and their special diets, and spend the next couple of weeks seeing the sights. Ladies: this might be a sport worth taking up.

'There's no middle ground – it's either win, or lose.' Words of deep wisdom from Sue Barker after an interview with Britain's great ping-pong hope.

SHIT

CRAP

DAY 2

A fragmented day: partly because I spent most of it on the phone to British Telecom, Official Supplier of the Internet to the Olympic Games, trying to get my broadband connection working again. It ultimately would take about a week, but at least this meant I could get some work done.

So here, rather than tidy up my notes, you get to see them, O privileged reader!, just as I typed them down in between listening to a selection of soothing classical music while on hold with BT.

Watery

Women cycling the same route – now in the rain

funny to be enduring the same weather

dutch have won twice

our first medal – Lizzie Armitstead (silver)

Paula Radcliffe pulling out of the marathon

US skeet shooting gold woman (had her gun stolen at Beijing)

women's synchronized diving (3m springboard), a sport whose chief excitement for the spectator, apart from, let us be honest about this, the sight of young athletic bodies in swimsuits, enacting something that faintly recalls the common male fantasy involving twins, resides in being on the look-out for someone smacking their head on the board. Not, of course, that one wants this to happen.

the British pair Alicia Blagg, Rebecca Galantree, described as 'holding their nerve' as they bounce from the boards; that is, at a point in the execution where you would have thought that freaking out had ceased to be an option. But this is a trope the commentator keeps returning to.

pysmenska fedorova, ukr 'nothing spectacular', but they did two and a half backwards turns at what seemed like twice the possible human speed, or, as I saw it, bloody spectacular. Then the Australian pair do three turns.

Commentator: 'There you go, pick the bones out of that one.' I try, and fail.

I missed the water polo, on the grounds that it is a very silly sport, but not actually silly enough to be entertaining.

Besides, I had to save myself in order to see how Rebecca Adlington does in the swimming. 'She's going to have to do it the hard way,' was how Gary Lineker evaluated how easily or not she was going to have to make history. Having barely qualified, she is going to be in the 'notorious lane 8'.

(Notorious, that is, not only for being the lane reserved for the lowest-qualified swimmer, but also for the fact that the backwash from all the other competitors, bouncing off the wall of the pool, disrupts the water – it's easier to swim through a calm than a choppy pool – and also minimizes the sightlines, so that it is hard to check on the progress of the other swimmers. The same applies, of course, to lane 1.) This is a kind of anti-handicapping, the conferring of advantage upon advantage to the already strongest swimmer. Is this unfair? It certainly seems to compromise one version of this year's Olympic Ideal, its 'diversity and inclusion'; but then moving the best swimmer to an outside lane would also, looked at another way (from the perspective that to the winner belong the spoils, which is what the Olympic Ideal really entails, like it or not), be 'unfair'.

Earlier on, Frankie Boyle, the comedian who makes a habit of saying 'controversial' things in – it must be whispered – possibly an attempt to raise his profile, caused a stink on Twitter by saying that Adlington might have an advantage because she has 'a face like a porpoise'. I hesitate to give the man further publicity, but we ought to acknowledge that the looks of the athletes are one of the selling points of the Games, and were so from the beginning, when the Greeks had oiled young men wrestling each other. But I begin to feel that maybe it is time for me to be rather more high-minded, particularly in the knowledge that Rick Dewsbury, the man who wrote what was generally agreed to be the most hateful article of all about the opening ceremony, had also, on 19 July, co-written an article for the *Daily Mail*, extensively illustrated by pictures of female beach volleyball players and the like, with the headline: 'The oh, oh, Ohhh-lympics! As a record 150,000 condoms are handed out to a host of super-attractive athletes, could London 2012 be the raunchiest games ever?' (Quotation from the body of the article, if we can dignify it with that description, is redundant.) I accept, reluctantly in this instance, that I am, as a hack, in the same business as this Dewsbury character, but there is a point at which professional solidarity breaks down, and I become amazed at how long it is possible for some of my fellow scribes to operate without a sense of shame.

Later on, I read a report on the *New Statesman* website which shows not all was well while the opening ceremony was going on:

> The police were arresting over 100 members of the cycling group, Critical Mass; a group which has been cycling together on London's streets for the last 18 years with no aim but to celebrate the joy of bikes. In the words of one cyclist who was arrested, 'I can honestly say I had absolutely zero intention of disrupting the Olympics. I don't think anyone did. It was about enjoying cycling – not hating the Olympics.'
>
> In 2008, the House of Lords had ruled that Critical Mass was acting completely lawfully and that the Metropolitan Police were not allowed to obstruct the bike rides. And yet, at around midnight on Friday the police ushered the cyclists into a cul-de-sac in East London, kettled them, and began forcing some off their bikes. Over 100 were then arrested under Section 12 of the Public Order Act. They were

bundled on coaches, where they remained for over 7 hours without access to food, water or toilets. One of the arrestees was a 13-year-old boy.

Arrestees were later released with stringent bail conditions, including a ban from cycling in an entire London borough, Newham.

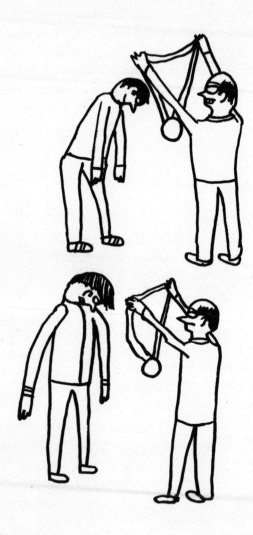

DAY 3

···

Key-losing
Horsing About
Tennis
Gym (pronounced, as Homer
Simpson does it, with a hard
'G', and to rhyme with 'time')

···

To the newsagents, and the screaming front page of the *Daily Mail* (in a disconcerting reversal of the order in the run-up to the Games, it is beginning to look as if the mainstream left and right are swapping roles as grumblers and boosters of the Games). 'OLYMPIC SECURITY FARCE AS WEMBLEY KEYS LOST' is the headline, and I have to say that this presents an aspect to large-scale mainstream sport in this country that I had never come close to imagining.

'Olympic security staff have lost the keys to Wembley Stadium,' ran the opening sentence of the report. 'A furious row erupted last night over who was to blame for the breach,' ran the second. This conjures an almost touching scene, a familiar domestic drama ('Well, where did you see them last?' 'How the fuck should I know?' 'Are you accusing me of losing them?', etc.), and the detail that the keys are not just ordinary keys, but 'high-tech laser keys' (whatever that is; I briefly envisage something along the lines of Doctor Who's sonic screwdriver) costing 'up to' £40,000 (presumably one gets a discount for bulk orders) only adds to the comedy. As does the idea that Wembley Stadium actually *has* keys. Well, I suppose it has to, doesn't it? Someone might sneak in one night and steal the turf.

Apparently, a set of keys to Wimbledon has gone missing, too. A G4S spokesman said, 'We have no record of losing any keys,' although it is in the nature of key-losing that you do not realize that you have lost them until it is too late to make a record of losing them. Unless they fall down a drain in plain sight, or an outraged lover snatches them from your grasp and hurls them into the river, you can't say, '23.15. Lost keys.' LOCOG say, with pardonable but unconvincing defensiveness, as defensiveness in these circumstances so often is: 'LOCOG has not lost any keys.'

'Have you looked in your jacket pocket?' 'Of course I looked there, you idiot, it was the first place I looked!' 'Well, look again,' etc., etc.

The talk on the television news, however, is all, or almost all, of empty seats. Well, of course, not even 'almost all', for there is plenty of other detail to be mulled over, but it is the most prominent item (the keys rating not a mention), and the recurrent image is that of four or five paratroopers sitting in a tidy row, isolated among a huge bank of empty seats. Were

I a spectator, I would be in two minds about these no-shows, who are said to be mainly members of the 'Olympic family', and so are in the most coveted areas. On the one hand, I would decry the loss of atmosphere and the insult to all those who really wanted tickets but never got any; on the other, I would at least console myself that the queues for food and toilets would be less lengthy. Reports from some of the venues in today's *Guardian* claim that some people are having to wait for hours in line before they can be served.

The cross-country equestrian event has been delayed. The horses are rebelling and throwing their human masters off them. This is it, I think: the first steps towards the establishment of the breakaway republic, the country of the Houyhnhnms, where reason is king and no lie can be told. Not for the first time, though, I find I have sleepwalked into a land of reverie, and the delay, it turns out, has been for reasons far more quotidian. Still, there is an element of fantasy to the course: the jumps echo the opening ceremony in their almost surreal evocation of an alternative, non-Olympic Britain: the cricket bats, Winnie-the-Pooh, Toad, a crescent moon, a pentagon (officially: the Diamond Jubilee Hedge). Later on, there is an interview with a so-far triumphant Zara Phillips. She doesn't sound that posh *at all*. I am impossibly disappointed. (However, at least she still looks like Zara Phillips, but when I close my eyes and try to imagine what I would usually expect someone with that voice to look like or come from, no one looking like Zara Phillips emerges from the mental identikit.) Later on, I watch a couple of riders fall off their horses after attempting what look like plainly unjumpable jumps: how *anyone* manages to negotiate this sinister horsey playground (imagine Portmeirion in *The Prisoner*, or one of the wackier episodes of the 60s' incarnation of *The Avengers*, but with more jumping) without coming a cropper is something I find hard to understand.

In between sailing events, we get a profile of Shirley Robinson: 'Born in Dundee, 32 years later, voted the greatest female sailor in the world.' The suggestion being that all you have to do to be considered the greatest female sailor in the world is to be born in Dundee and just wait.

There is a palpable sense of lack of occasion in the tennis – even though it's being played at Wimbledon; perhaps *because* it's being played at Wimbledon. We know what we're not getting, and the non-white outfits of the players make it look as though all they're doing is having a knock-up. And what with the keys having gone missing, and an opportunistic thief having stolen the nets and balls in the night, the players are improvising with picnic tables turned on their sides and balls made entirely of rubber bands, which adds a charm to the game it has lacked ever since the men's tournament abandoned long trousers. (These trips to the land of reverie will now stop.)

Louis Smith, we are told, is 'in floods of tears after his amazing performance on the pommel horse' – Sue Barker, with her reliable gift for the arresting juxtaposition. (And indeed, when we see his tears, we learn that she is not exaggerating.) The business with the pommel horse does look ... well,

I hesitate to say 'interesting', but it is certainly difficult and balletic, utterly pointless of course, as well as obviously requiring enormous upper-body strength. It is, however, for me, one of the more painful sports to watch – as well as the other gymnastic disciplines, the rings, the beam and the vault, for all these instruments of torture featured in the gyms of my youth. I remember well how at first they looked as though they might be fun to play on (apart, of course, from the beam, whose dauntingly narrow breadth straight away identified itself as something that was out to get me if I went anywhere near it); until one actually got to grips with the things. Then they quickly revealed themselves as engines devised for the humiliation of schoolboys, and this school-boy in particular. And this, mind you, was involving nothing more than either holding yourself up for a few panicky, gasp-ing seconds (the rings), or bouncing over the thing (the vault) or ... hang on, I would say to myself, what the hell is the pommel horse *for*? You could imagine sitting on it and pre-tending to ride it like a horse (it is, of course, deliberately designed to re-create mounting and dismounting techniques), but it doesn't bounce, swing, or move at all. Neither can you, as with the vault, use it to hide under while a couple of your confrères with makeshift spades dig a tunnel out of the bloody gym to freedom. Anyway. At Olympic level, I learn, on the high bar, 'triple twisting somersaults are considered almost routine'. Well, la-di-da. I don't think I could complete a triple twisting somersault on the ground, even if I had four years to prepare, and although some of the athletes in the gymnastics are performing moves of unbelievable grace and power, all they are really doing is making me think darkly about my own uncoordination and weakness, and so I slip off to the bookshop for a copy of *How to Watch the Olympics* (published by Penguin too, I note; it would seem my publisher is, with Machiavellian cunning, catering to all shades of reaction to the Games) and a bottle of wine from Waitrose.

Towards the evening, I find my head spinning with all the data, the swarm of impressions clashing not only with my imperative to write 1,500 or more meaningful words about the day's events, but my own indifference to many of the entirely and wilfully pointless sports. (There is also the matter of BT's Local Area Network broadband still being down, and the long time I am being kept on hold while someone tries to fix the problem, and irony number 27 involves, unsurprisingly, the fact that still, on Day 3, BT declares itself the official supplier of interwebs to the Olympics. It is a matter I bring up pointedly during my discussions with the various representatives I have to deal with.) It's all right for you and everyone else: you can let it all wash over you. I have to *pay attention*. To put this into a personal context: I learn from my copy of *How to Watch the Olympics* that 79 per cent of the population of the globe watched at least some of the 2008 Games: I didn't watch a single second of them, not even by mistake.

It is all starting to get too much, and by about seven in the evening I feel the serious need to unwind. 'Fuck this,' I say, in a shameful inversion of the Olympic ideal of *mens sana in corpore sano*, 'I'm going to get fucked up.' I roll myself an Interesting Cigarette and start pouring a bottle of red wine into me. 'It's deea foowa of the Olympics,' says my girlfriend, assuming the cadences of the Geordie voice-over of *Big Brother*, 'and Nicholas Lezard is gooing to get fooked up.' The next day she leaves for a holiday in Sweden, as I have advised her I am not going to be much fun to hang around with for the next fortnight. And I will be right.

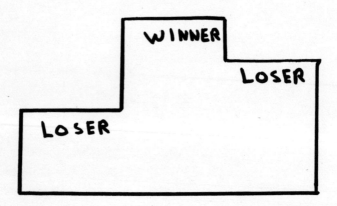

31 July 2012

DAY 4

·····································

Judo
Horsey Riding
Badminton
Nasty Tweeting
Gymnastics

·····································

The day dawns sodden from the night's rain, and with the knowledge sinking into the nation that Great Britain currently languishes in twentieth place in the medals table. This is seventeen places behind France, which makes Boris Johnson's very specific targeting of that nation as the one to beat look rather like a hostage to fortune.

The *scandale du matin*: a US coach (John Leonard, executive director of the World Swimming Coaches Association), has said Ye Shiwen, the sixteen-year-old who broke a swimming world record in the 400m medley, did so in a 'suspicious' way, i.e. through the illegal use of drugs. He doesn't say so outright, but his reference to Michelle Smith in Atlanta

1996 means he doesn't have to in order to make his meaning clear. Lord Moynihan, British Olympic Association chairman, says no she didn't, and the story should stop there. And that's that. The press gets behind Ye Shiwen, and we flatter ourselves that these are the most drug-free Games ever. This is a murkier area than we realize: not only are certain levels of steroids permitted to athletes, you have to wonder whether forcing young athletes, like rhubarb, to excel, is itself in the spirit. It is, of course, because Sparta did much the same kind of thing thousands of years ago that this seems even faintly reasonable, as did, throughout the ages, every militarized society with a reputation to maintain. But we are still treated, the next day, to a sidebar on the *Daily Mail*'s website, whose headline tells us all we need to know about this kind of attitude: 'Forging of the Mandarin mermaid: how Chinese children are taken away from their families and brutalized into future Olympians.' And, in case we miss the import, underneath: 'Ye Shiwen started at 7.'

While I listen to the hoo-ha about Ye Shiwen on the Radio 4 news, I see a Briton, Euan Burton, being thrown to the floor repeatedly by a Canadian, Valois, in the first round of the men's 81kg Judo. 'Clearly a very emotional moment right now,' says the commentator, sticking his microphone in the abject Burton's face, while the judoka tries to collect himself. He looks crushed with disappointment, on the verge of tears, very far from that emotional place where the usual post-match nostrums are best delivered. In a cruel inversion of the extravagantly grateful Oscar acceptance speech, Burton gives us an exhaustive list of all the people he feels he has let down. Here, perhaps, we glimpse the unforeseen downside of pre-Olympic hubris (which is not, in this case, his fault) – although this would not have been unforeseen to those who had absorbed the lesson of Gluteus Maximus's despair upon discovering that he was not, after all, the greatest.

'Was it a mistake?' asks this potential winner of Tactful Olympic Interviewer 2012, referring to the final throw which saw Burton also thrown out of the competition. No, says Burton, it was 'a beautiful bit of Judo – if I say it's a mistake it's a disservice to my opponent'. (I recall the little bow of respect the judokas make at the beginning of each match, which I must say on this occasion looked a little perfunctory; misleadingly so, as Burton's subsequent remarks, pregnant with honesty and grace, attest.) 'Can you take anything positive out of this experience?' he is asked, the interviewer unwisely grasping at straws in the face of the man's unambiguous misery. 'No,' replies Burton, without pausing for even a second.

Judo is yet another one of those sports of which I have some small personal experience. I suppose the reason I tried so many was in order to see if I discovered any that I hated playing less than football. How long did judo last? A couple of terms, as I recall, and I enrolled for the second one only because I was simply too stunned to accept that the first one had been so horrible. An undersized child for my years, always at the bottom end of the height scale in class, I was keen to find a means of leveraging my paltry strength into something better; to punch, so to speak, above my weight. What I really wanted to learn, like all boys in the 1970s, was kung fu, or at a pinch karate, one or both of these holding forth the promise of an ability to sever wooden planks with a well-timed sideways chop of the hand. Useful in a fight with the bullies either at one's own school or the state one down the road; and just the kind of thing that would impress the girls. But classes in kung fu (which we suspected was probably no more than a creation of certain tacky TV studios targeting the insecure male adolescent demographic) and karate were unavailable, and, as we were told in exasperation, neither of these disciplines could be approached without learning judo first.

The next four months of Tuesday and Thursday afternoons were all about being thrown to the floor by larger and, on plenty more than one occasion, smaller boys (it is around this time that I began to think that 'wiping the floor' with someone was more than just colourful metaphor). I had been assured several times that the point of judo was to use your opponent's strength against him, which had a certain appeal, on the grounds that this was, for me, the only way forward, given that pretty much everyone was stronger than me as far as I could see; but, of course, this is horse feathers, and all I really learned is that if someone stronger than you wants to throw you around a judo mat like a pizza base being thrown around by a show-off pizza cook, there is little you can do to prevent it. I vaguely recall a load of pseudo-spiritual bullshit attached to the sport, which I was usually too bruised to absorb, and I never progressed beyond the most pristine of white belts, all the while marvelling that a sport that made so much of its essentially pacific intent seemed to unleash some kind of frenzy in my opponents, and if I say no more about this wretched sport for the rest of this book, now you know the reason why. (Although, as it turns out, I will.)

★

Meanwhile, there is plenty of messing about on fancy nags today, even though the going is soft. Kristina Cook gets a silver medal in the horsey jumping, on behalf of the British horsey team.

Zara Phillips, I learn from the 2007 official biography by Brian Hoey (updated for paperback publication in 2008, by Virgin Books), is 'by her own admission . . . not an academic', but she knuckled down to do her exams, even after getting her tongue pierced while at Gordonstoun (showing it off at her uncle Charles's fiftieth birthday do; discipline, it would appear, is laxer at the school than it was in his day), to gain a place at Exeter ('one of the best universities in England') to study for a diploma in equine physiotherapy. In making horses her life and work, she is obviously her mother's daughter. This fondly recalls Prince Philip's words, before Princess Ann's marriage to Mark Phillips, about the difficulty of finding a prospective mate for her: 'If it doesn't fart and eat hay, she isn't interested.'

Zara is riding Clifton Promise in the Individual Horseying (and High Kingdom in the Team Horseying: apparently, she nearly cost us a medal in the team event, when she knocked a pole off a jump, but the commentators later reassure us, in order to forestall a republican uprising, that this had no bearing on the result at all). We also learn that Miner's Frolic, Tina Wilson's horsey, which I must say bucks the trend for regally inspired names among Team GB's horseys, nearly died last year, needing loads of blood transfusions. (Where, I wonder, do they get the blood from? Do the horses volunteer? Or, like blood donors in America, are they paid?) And finally, once the showjumping is over, the commentator pays a compliment to the horse, which makes me wonder for a second if it might not improve the sport simply to let the horses, who after all are the ones doing all the jumping and running, get on with it on their own. I've seen what happens when a horse unseats its rider in the Grand National: it streaks ahead and beats everyone else. Only some quirk of the rules disqualifies them. Which strikes me as unfair, for the last time I checked, when a horse runs a race it does so under its own name, not that of the little chap on its back.

'Such a lovely young lady,' says the commentator of Phillips as she accepts her silver medal. This is actually the first medal ceremony I have paid close attention to, for some reason, and I notice that the medals are a lot bigger than I thought they were going to be.

Anyway, there are fifteen people on that podium accepting medals, and as far as I can see, just about all of them look like horses. But not in a bad way, of course. I saw Britain's great canoeing hope being interviewed earlier, and I thought for a few seconds that she looked like a canoe, which is clearly impossible. I am just mapping my own prejudices and knowledge of the sport the athletes are competing in onto my own perceptions. Would we have done better in the archery if more of our archers had looked like Robin Hood? Or been called 'Archer'?

Ouseph of Great Britain, who had been leading 14–11 in the final game in the badminton, manages to get knocked out by Corden of Guatemala (which, as we are reminded, has a scant-to-zero history of achievement, at any level, in the sport). Badminton: there is another sport dragged out of the dimmer recesses of the memory banks. The historical origins of this sport, as far as I am concerned, lie in the back garden of my parents' house in East Finchley in the early 1970s. I used to fancy myself as being rather nifty at this, with our ancient, tattered net strung up between the cherry tree and the fence-post, and my opponents consisting chiefly of my mother, well-preserved but, largely because of the lack in her of anything like the sporting competitive spirit, uncommitted, and my brother, five years younger than me, and easily intimidated. My father, the natural sportsman, was stiffer competition, at forty-three, even though a tad overweight and steadfastly progressing towards his first heart attack. The object of the game, whose scoring system I still remember, was to whack the shuttlecock as hard as you could so that it landed squarely between my little brother's eyes.

Meanwhile, a seventeen-year-old boy has been arrested for posting a mean tweet about Tom Daley, saying that his failure to win a medal in the 10m diving would have disappointed his late father, who died of brain cancer a year ago. Clearly a horribly unpleasant thing to say, and the product of a disturbed and negligible mind, but I do wonder whether this is an arrestable offence.

In the afternoon, there is a brief interview with Olga Korbut, who, what with the passage of time and all that, is not looking quite as young as she did when she sent the world into a paroxysm of frankly disturbing appreciation of the pubescent female form. Her co-presenter, with a fumbling attempt at gallantry that would not impress the judges were it an

Olympic discipline, says that she still has the smile of her youth. (The impression he leaves, of course, is that everything else about her has gone to pot.)

There is then a short public information lesson about the beam, which, although clearly demonstrating the fact that you have to be preternaturally coordinated just to climb onto the bloody thing, let alone perform the mandatory flying somersault on it, is then followed by the necessary information should we wish to 'get involved' with the sport. No, I think to myself, not this one either.

Medal table: despite a couple of baubles today so far (I write this about 4.30 in the afternoon), we are still at number 20 in the medals table, or, to put some perspective on the matter, eleven places behind Kazakhstan. (Six o'clock update: Kazakhstan has moved up to 6 in the medals table, 'we' have moved down to 21.)

In other news: 600 million people in India – about half the population – are without electricity, which rather puts my problems with BT Broadband into perspective.

And the evening news is full of London stallholders with stories about how this is their worst July ever: even right next to the venues, visitors are being herded away from local businesses. We are shown a sign put up in front of a pub saying: 'Locog: licence to kill a town centre'. They make a further point by using a good approximation of the annoying official typeface of the Olympic Games 2012 (infantilia sans serif).

1 August 2012

DAY 5

····························

LOCOG
Rowing
Cycling

····························

RULE 40 FROM THE OLYMPIC CHARTER

Except as permitted by the IOC Executive Board, no competitor, coach, trainer or official who participates in the Olympic Games may allow his person, name, picture or sports performances to be used for advertising purposes during the Olympic Games.

THE BRIEFING NOTE SENT OUT TO ATHLETES BY LOCOG

Ambush marketers have, in the past, used their association with athletes to suggest or imply that they have an association with the Olympic Games. This undermines the exclusivity that Organising Committees can offer official Games and Team sponsors, without whose investment the Games could not happen.

The implication of an association with the Games through use of athletes is particularly powerful during and immediately before the Games.

It adds: 'Participants who do not comply with Rule 40 may be sanctioned by the IOC and/or by the BOA in accordance with the Team Members' Agreement which provides for wide ranging sanctions, including amongst other things removal of accreditation and financial penalties.'

I quote this officialese because (a) it is currently a major cause of contention between LOCOG and American athletes, who are collectively as mad as an Olympic team of wet hens because they can't pose for photos in which their non-accredited sponsors' products can be displayed, and (b) because that word 'exclusivity' rather flatly contradicts that word 'inclusivity' which, in LOCOG's propaganda, made so many people snort with derision.

I am sent, kindly, and generously, a book by Faber: *Winning Words: Inspiring Poems for Everyday Life*. A handwritten note wryly alerts me to its relevance. Leafing through it I come across a poem by Hafez, which runs, in its entirety, thus:

My Brilliant Image

I wish I could show you
When you are lonely or in darkness,

The Astonishing Light
Of your own Being!

I am reminded of the sample of poetry given in the P. G. Wodehouse story 'The Aunt and the Sluggard', a Jeeves story from the mid-1920s, which tells of Bertie Wooster's poet friend, the fabulously indolent Rocky Todd, who, with pardonable opportunism, writes lines like this:

> Be!
> Be!
>> The past is dead,
>> Tomorrow is not yet born.
>> Be today!
> Today!
>> Be with every nerve,
>> With every fibre,
>> With every drop of your red blood!
> Be!
> Be!

This poem appears in print with a picture 'of a fairly nude chappie with bulging muscles giving the rising sun the glad eye'. Wodehouse, who actually revered sport in real life, stood for no oompus-boompus when it came to connecting laughable art with Corinthian ideals (we have here an early example of the totalitarian drive to connect physical prowess with moral worth). Bertie adds the further gloss: 'Rocky said they gave him a hundred dollars for it, and he stayed in bed till four in the afternoon for the following month.'

There is, at lunchtime, finally a British gold: the women's pairs. This is rowing. One of my gripes about athletes is that in order to be contenders they have to have started training pretty much immediately after having learned to walk, but Helen Glover didn't take up rowing until about four years ago, and, moreover, is an inch below the minimum height requirement for those wishing to learn. And her co-rower is an army officer. ('The very middle-class supergirls' runs the approving headline in the *Daily Mail* the next day, although 'middle-class' is now elastic enough a term to include Gordonstoun-educated girls like Zara P. and Captain Heather Stanning.) The commentary at the moment illustrates once more the cruelly exacting demands being made on the vocabulary of the British sporting journalist. 'It [the gold] couldn't have gone to two worthy, worthy women.' There is a very small pause between the two 'worthy's, as if he knows he has not really quite got there the first time; but, unable to summon the resources for the last big push, sticks with the first one. (I assume that his grammar is betraying him, and he does in fact consider the women worthy.) I am not going to mock: this, the repetition of the wrong word, is a verbal glitch I once suffered from, unforgettably, more than thirty years ago. A girl I had been pursuing for months at university finally, despite all the odds stacked against me, finally agreed to climb into my bed. My brain scrambled through drink, elation and the sheer effort involved in getting her there in the first place, I murmured her name into her ear as I held her; from the way she stiffened I was at once aware I had picked the wrong one. My mind froze, and so I had another go; only with the same name, again. But her name had not changed in the interval between my two endearments, and she got dressed and left, and later on married someone far more suitable, i.e. someone gallant enough to remember what she was called, so I suppose everything turned out all right in the end.

The *Sun*, this morning, has printed a pair of '24-carat' sideburns, in emulation of the British champion cyclist, Bradley Wiggins, who is racing in the 44km time trial today. 'GOING FOR WIGGOLD' runs the front-page headline. On page 5, a blonde woman, presumably some luckless internee, models the sideburns for the benefit of the paper's readership. ('Be a hair-o.') 'Affixing your Wiggo sideburns is furry simple. Step 1: Cut along the dotted lines. Step 2: Double over Sellotape and stick to the back (do not use glue). Step 3: Gently press sideburns to face. Step 4: Cheer on Wiggo!'

A Venezuelan finishes the course in fifty-seven minutes and five seconds. I wonder how long it would take me to complete the route. As I no longer possess a racing bike – there is an ancient women's Peugeot which I used for years but it now rusts on the back terrace – I have to calculate using the only figures I have available: viz. how long it takes me to cycle to the British Library from my home on a Boris bike. (Once the idea enters my head that it would be simply wonderful to stage all the London 2012 cycling events on Boris bikes, it does not leave.) Wiggins is averaging 51.6 km/h so far, which I think means he could do the roughly three-mile run in about five or six minutes; I manage it in a stately fifteen or so. Well, twenty, really. But those Boris bikes have sacrificed speed to sturdiness, and I also often obey traffic lights. ('He's got wings on his wheels, has Bradley Wiggins,' says the commentator, which partly explains the difference in our cycling speeds. You see, I don't.)

I am fascinated by the freakish aerodynamic posture cyclists are obliged to adopt – assuming the form of a human teardrop; it must be murder on the back. Froome, even without his helmet, looks as though he has been formed in a wind tunnel, licked into shape, as it were, by his sport.

(Are those *golden thrones* on the podium?? Dear God, they are, but it transpires they are a staging post on the way to the podium proper; when winners accept their medals, the music from *Chariots of Fire* is played, notwithstanding the devastation the tune has had visited upon it by Rowan Atkinson's skit during the opening ceremony.)

I have to admit that, as Wiggins inexorably approaches the finish line, I am suffused with anxiety lest he ride into a bollard, or some twerp of a spectator dash out and try to hug him; at one point he cycles perilously close to a flag some idiot has dropped on the road. My legs pump involuntarily beneath my chair. The victory (and Froome's bronze) finally take us up to the top ten in the medals table, but we still languish behind Kazakhstan, although only in terms of gold medals won, not in terms of medals overall. (By the end of the evening, it transpires we have leapfrogged that much-maligned-by-Sasha-Baron-Cohen nation, and I hope they pull their socks up later. It would be an excellent rebuke for the derision they have suffered at his hands over the years.)

The *Sun* has a report about Reece Messer, the teenager who insulted Tom Daley on Twitter: his father, Norman, has apologized profusely. It appears that Reece has ADHD 'but doesn't take his medicine'. Reece (who, it seems, has ten siblings; the *Sun* imparts this information as an aside, a moment of untypically delicate restraint, you might think, although they may capitalize on this later on) also tweeted, afterwards: 'I'm going to drown you in the pool you cocky t*** your [sic] a nobody.' I feel reluctant to wag the finger here, given that there is an illustration in this book somewhere of a cyclist with that very asterisked word, un-asterisked, adorning his helmet, but in our defence this was drawn before Bradley Wiggins became the greatest Briton who ever lived, and besides does not represent any cyclist in particular, but is just one artist's expression of his frustration at the cult of sportsmanship.

This is something particularly on my mind today, as last night I was sent an email whose first word was 'URGENT' from Radio 4, asking me to be a guest on *The Moral Maze*. For those of you unfamiliar with it, this programme takes a topical issue and debates it in front of a panel composed of one herbivorous liberal, one person of indeterminate opinions, and two foaming, barking, swivel-eyed right-wingers and/or libertarians, usually Melanie Phillips, an ex-left-winger who now enjoys a reputation as a scourge of Political Correctness, and Claire Fox, the chair of the laughably named Institute of Ideas, which carefully cultivates a reputation as a scourge of Political Correctness. There is some confusion as to which of them is the more unpleasant, but Phillips certainly takes the biscuit as the more crazy of the two, at least on the surface. (Fox, who has championed such causes as denial of Serbian prison camps and the right to look at child pornography online, may well have the more warped mind, but she is not as much of a spittle-flecker in her delivery.)

I have long yearned to lock horns with either of these maniacs, and so when I am asked to contribute to a debate on how moral sport is, I start practising my thoughts, and my suave and witty put-downs. I have a *mauvais quart d'heure* when I contemplate the possibility that Phillips and Fox, noted contrarians, may well take roughly the same position that I propose to adopt, but my own arguments, as I rehearse them, are unalterable. Sport, I say to the researcher down the phone in the morning, is ethically neutral. True, there may be splendid individual moments of sporting magnanimity and decency, but these are more than offset by examples of greed, hubris and sheer unpleasantness from both players and spectators. The quintessential, primal example of athletic competition, I say, is two boys racing each other to that tree at the end of the road; to say that the one who reaches it first is morally the superior of the one who reaches it second is nonsensical and a reversion to the medieval days when disputes were settled by combat, the winner being, in effect, ordained by God, and the loser just having to lump it. Warming to my theme, I add that 'sport', until the word came along in the late seventeenth century, was what we said when we meant 'fun', and 'sport' still retains a whiff of that meaning even now; but if someone had started on about the ethics of fun, we would assume he had lost his marbles or, more charitably, had made what philosophers politely call a category error. I am asked whether it is true that sport contributes to 'self-knowledge'. This bamboozles me completely. The only self-knowledge I have gained from having played any kind of sport is 'I'm not terribly good at this'. Am I then meant to decide that all those years reading Shakespeare, Nietzsche, Schopenhauer, Plato, Beckett or the *Evening Standard* have contributed less to my, or anyone else's, self-knowledge than if we'd spent more time trying to become Olympians?

Later on in the morning, I am rung up by the production team and told that they are going to have to stand me down, as they have found someone to appear who has actually won an Olympic medal. I make a nasty comment about athletes being famously articulate, and go back to bed for a bit.

Later on, we see the badminton players from Korea (South and North) and China and Indonesia admit they played to lose: serving deliberately into the net in order to gain easier passage to the next round. Even the brief clips are dismaying, and strongly against the spirit of the Game when the rules were codified in East Finchley in 1973.

'So magical, that setting, this castle, wherever we are' (waves vaguely in the direction of Hampton Court). 'So British.' – Bradley Wiggins in his post-medal ceremony interview.

Lord Sebastian Coe says that Michael Phelps – with nineteen Olympic medals to his name – is probably not the greatest Olympian of all time. This seems ungenerous even before someone else points out that maybe that accolade should belong to Jesse Owens.

★

Unnamed Australians on our rowing triumph: the British are great at sports where you're sitting down. I'm fine with this. (Although this is a bit rich of them, seeing as one of the few sports for which they hold a gold medal involves the use of bicycles, which you have to sit on to make them work.)

In other news: Gore Vidal dies. The official cause of death given is pneumonia, but it may also possibly have been boredom.

And later on in the evening, I tune in to *The Moral Maze*. 'The thing about sport,' says one of the guests, 'is that it is ethically neutral.'

2 August 2012

DAY 6

....

Comedy politics
Double Trap
Judo
Canoeing

....

The political ramifications of the Olympics are becoming harder and harder to ignore. There is now, officially, no one alive who says that politics and sport shouldn't mix. Boy, do they mix. They mix like gin and tonic. The latest excitement, all over the papers this morning, involves, yet again, our good friend Boris the Johnson. In his latest, possibly inadvertent publicity stunt, he was going down a zip-wire in Victoria Park when he got stuck, and was left dangling, for all the world like a comedy David Blaine, thirty feet above the ground for ten minutes. 'Is it a bird?' asked a member of the gathering crowd. 'No, it's a buffoon,' came one reply, but buffoonery is to Johnson what the briar patch was to Brer Rabbit, and he milked it for all it was worth. (Someone with no dignity has nothing to lose in such a situation.)

David Cameron, who is losing whatever grip he had on public affections by the minute as the Games progress – he is now semi-officially regarded as a jinx on any of the sports where he cheers on a hopeful Brit, none of whom so far have had to step on any part of the winners' podium when he has been attending – had to say, presumably through gritted teeth, 'if any other politician anywhere else in the world was stuck on a zip-wire it would be a disaster. For Boris, it's an absolute triumph.'

But there is a more serious matter for Johnson: his pre-recorded announcements urging Londoners to steer clear of London while the Games are on have proved all too successful, and reports are coming in from all over the capital of catastrophic slumps in revenue, as restaurants, theatres, cinemas and black cabs find their takings down by a minimum of 30 per cent.

There is, at least, more triumph for medallists, and it finally begins to look as though we have a chance, today, of really overtaking Kazakhstan: the lightweight coxless four get silver. 'A sterling effort from them,' says the presenter in her summary, 'sterling silver, in fact.' I am beginning, a mere six days into the events, to weary of this trope.

To lift my mood I check to see what inspirational poem there is in *Winning Words* (Faber and Faber, £7.99) for me today. How about Robert Frost's 'Riders', where he writes the attractive couplet:

> The surest thing there is is we are riders,
> And though none too successful at it, guiders . . .

Hmm.

I am mildly annoyed to miss the Azerbaijani bantamweight being declared the winner of his bout against a Japanese boxer, despite having been knocked to the canvas six times. Then again, I'm not that annoyed, for to gain the fullest pleasure from the cock-up I would have had to have watched the match, and as I get older, the spectacle of people hitting each other becomes ever less attractive. But this revolutionary judging method fails to catch on; the crowd boo loudly, and the decision is overturned.

I am a bit more annoyed to miss most of the table-tennis, because it is one of those sports that I find pleasing to play and only tolerably dispiriting to watch. I have no illusions about my ability to play table-tennis, but as long as I can beat my children that's good enough for me. These people are incredible, even if their gurns and bellows of triumph after each won point do little to recall the origins of the game, in which bored British officers stationed in India or Afghanistan would carve a champagne cork into a ball, and make a net out of cigar boxes. (This is actually true for once, the reality being so pleasantly surreal that there is little point in making up something ludicrous.)

Shooting is also, regrettably, brilliant. Goodness me, yet another sport I have personal experience of. I always preferred target shooting with a Martini, for you did that lying down (a sport you do *lying down*! That is wonderful), imagining unpopular masters' faces imposed on the targets, but rapid-fire pistol shooting, which you had to haul yourself to your feet and stand up for, was also fun. I had a go once, and was gratifyingly asked if that had really been the first time I'd ever done it, but decided in the end that my spare time at university would be better spent getting drunk and trying to get laid, as opposed to honing my technique at the Small Bore Club. I remember after the crackdown on guns following the Dunblane massacre the shooting lobby wailed that their own responsible competitive shooters would be unable to engage in their chosen sport. And yet, despite the (commendable) restrictions on owning firearms, we are still the land that nurtured Peter Wilson, Britain's top shooter, and, until three in the afternoon, at least, top of the world.

Shooting, in the double trap at least, is paradoxically soothing to watch. The clays explode in puffs of pinky-orange smoke (there is little point in the BBC showing these in slow-motion apart from the sheer boyish delight in it), and the shooters themselves look more like normal blokes than any other athletes I've seen in the Games so far. The Hungarian, Bognar, looks so Hungarian that I guess his nationality before I confirm it; I can just see him in a goulash-stained waistcoat going after boar in some central European forest; and Dahlby of Sweden looks positively *round*. You will also be delighted to learn, as I was, that according to the record books, Oscar Swahn of Sweden became, at the age of seventy-two, the oldest medallist ever, in the running deer event, bagging a silver at the 1920 Antwerp Games. (Not real deer: moving targets made of cardboard, and alas, the event no longer features.) It is also ridiculously simple in terms of scoring: you get a point if you hit a clay, you don't if you miss.

It's squeaky bum time as Wilson's lead starts slipping. Then he gets it back; then, astonishingly, misses two clays at once. Shooters, though, are not the most demonstrative of sportsmen – you don't really go waving your arms around when you've got a double-barrelled shotgun in your hands – and histrionics either in victory or defeat are eschewed. (Although Bognar, out of the reckoning by then, throws his cartridge into the bin after his 198th shot with a distinctly grumpy air, and the Swede runs around with his gun over his head when celebrating his silver.) Wilson wins: it goes to the last brace of shots, and after a tense match in which he is so restrained that all his face has registered when missing is the expression that goes with the muttered 'tsk!', he looks as though he is going to cry when he wins. I think we're ahead of Kazakhstan now.

Vladimir Putin, friend of the Syrian regime and jailer of Pussy Riot, arrived in town for the judo, of which he is an aficionado. This does not help endear me further to the sport. Marhinde Verkerk, the Dutch female judo wrestler, although placed only tenth in the world, scares the pants off me even before she's started fighting. She's up against the young British hopeful Gemma Gibbons (whatever the sport is, they're always 'hopeful', aren't they? Why aren't they ever described as being 'resigned to the inevitable'?), in a manner strongly suggestive of two women out of their minds on Red Bull and tequila having it out over a bloke in a Thurrock pub car park at chucking-out time. Turn the sound down and you can hear the guffaws of their lager-fuelled consorts. This, I admit, is an unpleasantly sexist and patronizing observation, not to mention an unpardonable libel against the good people of Thurrock,* compounded by my own reluctance to relearn even the little I ever knew about the sport, but I can't shake it. I do very much hope, though, that neither Verkerk nor Gibbons (who gets through to the semi-finals as I watch) reads these words, for it is abundantly clear that if they got me by the lapels in a pub car park in Thurrock at closing time, they'd reduce me to a smear on the tarmac within five seconds.

We learn that Gibbons's boyfriend is Euan Burton, the judoka who got so horribly thrown out of the competition a couple of days ago. Wow! Imagine what their home life must be like. Imagine if they have a disagreement about whose turn it is to do the dishes. (As I write, Gibbons has just got through to the finals, so I would imagine it is Mr Burton who reaches for the yellow gloves.)

Later on – not much later on, only about fifteen minutes, some of which includes a short lesson on the terms involved in judo – I see exactly the same pair of women fighting again. Only this time they are on the Brazilian and American teams. The physical resemblance to the previous pair is astonishing. Is this a rule they don't explain? That all bouts between

---

* According to a recent survey from the same company which tells us of the lavatory habits of bears and the religious observances of popes, Thurrock is the most miserable place in the country, so maybe there is something to my *jeu d'esprit*. Whatever they can do to pass the time, I suppose. The venerable comic 2000 AD once proposed, in one of its inspired satires, that sex be a future Olympic sport – if not the basis for an entire, separate Olympics; and I wonder whether one day dogging might be considered a possible sport. It would give Thurrock some hope.

women must be between an angry brunette with a top-knot in white pyjamas and an angry streaked blonde in blue pyjamas? The angry brunette scores a waza-mata against the American, which involves jamming an empty Breezer bottle in her eye, but the blonde replies with a magnificent hoki-coki, in which your opponent's face is pushed into a puddle of sump oil from a knackered Vauxhall Viva.

There is more canoeing. There has been so much canoeing that I have come, finally, to understand, unbidden, the difference between a canoe and a kayak. (The canoe is propelled, from a kneeling position, by a single-bladed paddle; the kayak is propelled by . . . you know what? I don't really care. I do know, but for all the difference this knowledge will make to my life, it might as well be propelled by a double-ended banjo wielded by an inbred yokel whistling the theme to *Deliverance*.) But it is a sport that firmly refuses to engage me. In fact, I actively dislike it. Canoeing should be done by Red Indians carrying tomahawks or not at all, and as for kayaking, any sport that involves wearing a 'skirt' has a problem as far as I'm concerned. Canoeing through rapids is just insane, and the notion that it is not only grudgingly accepted, but admitted as a matter of course, that when in a kayak you will be turned upside down and be forced to flip yourself back upright before you drown makes it an absolute, perpetual no-no. But we have been told that all of Slovakia has ground to a halt because the world champions, the Hochschorner twins, are in a paired canoe. Isn't it cheating a bit to be twins when you're both in the same canoe? Anyway, they don't do as well as everyone thought they were going

63

to. We win gold and silver, and there's a French canoeist out there crying like a baby. Kazakhstan declares a national day of mourning.

'Every so often, rubbish things happen' – Victoria Pendleton's winningly upbeat reaction to being disqualified in the women's cycling, thanks to an infringement of some obscure law about overtaking by her partner.

In other news: the Eurozone sneaks off to a corner where no one can see it, and quietly unravels.

3 August 2012

DAY 7

....

Cricket
Horsey Dancing
Class Treason

....

So: South Africa have started the second day of the second Test on 262 for 5, with Alviro Petersen on 124 and Jacques Rudolph on 1. The new ball is only seven overs old, so there is a chance for England's seamers – they have omitted a specialist spin bowler from their team, for reasons arcane but possibly connected to either the weather forecast, the state of Graeme Swann's elbow or both. But Swann, although not quite the force he was, is still England's leading wicket-taker, as well as being a handy bat and a reliable pair of hands in the slip-cordon.

Sorry, did I stray from the Olympics there for a bit? Was that paragraph incomprehensible? Or do you see it as a drop of sanity in an ocean of madness?

As I have already mentioned, it was interesting that when Danny Boyle's fantasy of Britain touched on sport, it very clearly avoided mentioning any connected with the Olympics. As well as showing clips of rugby tries from Wales and Scotland, there was an anachronistically mixed-race team in early nineteenth-century costume playing a game (anachronistically, with three stumps) on a stylized village green. Fine, I thought; and I still do. I will put up with the odd detail out of time for the implicit message: here is something that we do, that we invented, and in its leisurely pace and idiosyncratic make-up is something far removed from the frenetic and single-minded athleticism of the games that comprise the Olympics. You can still shock Americans when you tell them that at the highest level, games between well-matched teams last for five days, of seven hours play a day, with breaks for lunch and tea. Tea!

It is a game that is forgiving of the overweight, the tiny, the lanky, the weedy, the unathletic. One of my favourite players ever, the Middlesex and England spinner Phil Tufnell, when placed in the field somewhere on the boundary and therefore far enough out of the way not to do much damage to the team by his own inept fielding, would regularly happily smoke cigarettes during those long intervals when the ball would fail to pick him out. (This proximity to the crowd had its drawbacks, mainly in Australia. 'Oy, Tuffers,' said one wag, 'we're building an idiot, give us your brain.' Most untypically for a remark bellowed out from an Australian crowd, this was unfair, however droll, for Tufnell is now a commentator, and has revealed himself as a shrewd and articulate explicator of the game. Shame on you, anonymous Australian Frankenstein!) With the ball in his hand, though, he was transformed. If you are good enough at any one of the three main disciplines of the game – batting, bowling or (to a lesser degree) fielding – you're in. At the village level, being able to walk unaided will be enough to qualify you for some teams. In its extraordinary complexity, in which it helps not only to be well coordinated, but to be part meteorologist, groundsman, psychologist and chess player, it acknowledges the cerebral – one England captain, Mike Brearley, was given the job despite the steady decline of his batting ability, because he was simply so good at it. He had a first-class degree from Cambridge, and was as posh as they come (well, almost, for cricket has absorbed an awful lot of poshness); but he knew how to get the best out of his team, including the wayward but big-hearted genius Ian Botham, who had been given a shot at the job himself and had failed dismally.* The story of the 1981 series against the Australians, as the visitors had victory yanked from their grasp by a series of incredible English acts of daring, is one known by heart by all England fans, and any who are reading these words will not mock me if I say that I find that a lump seems to have lodged itself in my throat as I write them.

* A. G. Macdonell's *England, Their England*, a novel best remembered today for its much-anthologized chapter dealing with a village cricket match, ends with a vision of Shakespeare and Falstaff as the embodiment of the two prominent strains of the English – the sly, quiet, self-effacing genius, and the big, jolly comedy oaf – and, broadly speaking, this is a pattern that fits the Brearley/Botham relationship rather nicely. For all that they came from hugely differing backgrounds, they meshed together on the cricket pitch perfectly.

So a break from the Olympics, to watch a sport which has, for the spectator at least, great depth, seemed in order. But . . .

Partly because I do not want to pay their exorbitant fees, and partly because I loathe Rupert Murdoch, I do not have a Sky subscription, which means that I cannot watch live cricket on television, and neither has anyone else who shares my views been able to since 2006. We rely on the highlights, currently shown on Channel 5, in which seven hours of play are compressed into one, therefore robbing us of the sense of changing tempo that is one of the game's cherished features; or we go back to the 1930s, and listen to it on the radio, and if you listen to it on long wave rather than online the sense of backward time-travel is enhanced by the inferior sound quality (and if you have the radio on while writing on a computer, you have to put the radio at least six feet away from the machine, as whatever is going on inside the machine's innards serves to scramble the long-wave signal to unlistenability).

The commentary is legendary: a mixture of ex-players and patrician experts, with an inexhaustible ability to chunter on during long rain-breaks about cakes and pigeons and buses going by, and anything. (The poshest of these, and by some distance the most interested in buses, is the greatly beloved Henry Blofeld, son of the man who gave Ian Fleming the name of his most enduring villain. The novelist Tom McCarthy, a great cricket fan, to the extent that it intelligently infiltrates some of his fiction, once audaciously explained to Blofeld why it was that he went on about buses so much: because an accident with one had ended his own promising cricket-playing career. 'My dear chap,' said

Blofeld – these might not be his exact words, but that's how he talks* – 'I can't say I'd thought about it, but you might be onto something there.')

After the colour and flash and speed of the last week, I suddenly find myself in another world. I am fond of saying that cricket isn't a sport, it's a state of mind, but that flippant observation would seem to have some force. Its pace now suddenly seems glacial, as the South African batsmen block and grind their way to a daunting first-innings total. For a fleeting moment, I begin to understand why so many nations are not so much baffled as positively *outraged* that such an anti-sport should have any kind of following at all.

And although cricket has a reputation of being the last gentlemanly sport, untainted by corruption, greed or ungenerous behaviour to opposing teams, this reputation has not only been eroded drastically over the years, it never really bore much scrutiny in the first place. I might decry the monetization of its large spaces, whether on the green of the field, or the white of the players' clothes and the sight-screens, and the way you now have to pay through the nose to watch it, but I have to remind myself that the game became popular not so much because of the inherent thrill of trying to knock down some sticks with a ball, but because it is more or less tailor-made for gambling. And gambling has provided the game's most recent grave crisis: Pakistani players have been paid large sums to bowl illegal deliveries at specific times,

---

* Subsequent correspondence between myself and McCarthy elicited the information that what Blofeld actually said was 'My dear old thing'.

in order to satisfy the demands of continent-wide gambling syndicates.*

All of which is by way of saying that, mired in scandal though the Olympics have been at times, nothing sublunar is perfect, that just in the way all dogs look different but are still immediately identifiable as dogs, so cricket, while look-ing nothing like, say, the triple jump, is still, unavoidably, a sport, and that perhaps once every four years isn't so bad to make the switch and watch a load of running and jumping and throwing things, or people punching people or throwing them onto judo mats or blowing discs of clay to bits with a shotgun, and, besides, South Africa are just going on and on and on, and the only England bowler doing anything is Kevin Pietersen, who's not even a proper bowler (and, although technically English, or English enough to get into the team, he speaks with as broad a Saffer accent as you will ever hear).† So it's back to the Games, and the yachts off Weymouth are looking awfully pretty. And look: it's more horsey dancing! I never noticed that darling little white fence they have for it, which adds to the oddity and charm of the event, although even after what seems like hours of watching

* Cricket has actually been an Olympic sport, but only two teams have ever contested it in such a context: England and France, in 1908, the latter team comprised of English embassy staff. They lost, but France can always console itself with the knowledge that whatever happens to their country, they are the proud possessors of a silver medal in the game.

† In a phenomenon which will be familiar to all sports fans, my turning the radio off occasioned a flurry of actually eventful gameplay in England's favour.

the sport, I haven't the faintest idea what anyone is meant to do in it and what not to do, apart from not fall off. The horsey I am watching, I gather, has a nickname: Blueberry. That's funny, I thought all horsey names were, essentially, nicknames already. Perhaps this one is so well-bred that it's actually called Princess von Schleswig-Holstein de Montfort Sebag-ffytche-Montefiore, and 'Blueberry' just happens to roll more easily off the tongue.

This brings us neatly to the issue that always bubbles under just about every argument in this country, the Tiresome Subject: class. It is tiresome because it just won't go away, not even here. Lord Moynihan, who so far has been more sensible than most people expected him to be, has declared that the fact that half the British Olympics winners in 2008 were privately educated is 'one of the worst statistics in British sport', and it looks as though the pattern will be replicated here. The *Daily Telegraph*, which considers the British public school system one of the glories of the world, is always on the lookout for class treachery of this kind, and says in a leader this morning that, by such logic, Old Etonian medal-holders would be forced to hand back their gongs and their rowing lake over to *hoi polloi*. (They don't put it exactly like that, but I give you the gist.)

But Moynihan has a point, and it seems as though he really believes it, and isn't just parroting the rhetoric of egalitarianism, as Tories so often do when they want to stop looking too obviously like the party of privilege. There is a massive imbalance in resources when the state and private sectors are compared. (The attentive reader will have been able to deduce, from my declared familiarity with such 'elite' sports as shooting, judo, the fucking pommel horse, badminton, fencing – see tomorrow – and setting man-traps for poachers on my estate, that I am a product of the private system; by a curious spin-off of the class structure of the country, this means my anti-public school sentiments will be seen as tainted by people both sympathetic and antagonistic to them.) That our judo and shooting champions, or near-champions, are in fact not toffs throws an added degree of confusion into the mix. And as I write these words, Princes William and Harry are being interviewed on BBC1, and being asked at some length about their gran's skit with James Bond. If they consider her pretend jump from a helicopter an affront to her dignity, they're not letting on. Ah, and now they're talking about cousin Zara. These are dark days indeed for bolshie republicans like myself. As Peter Wilby has noted, if all secondary schools in this country had as much space devoted to buildings and sports grounds as Wellington College, pretty much every building in the land would have to be demolished to make room for them.

So it ill behoves the *Daily Mail* and others to complain about the way Chinese athletes are taken away from their parents to train for Olympic greatness at the age of seven. The difference here is that we send our children away to these training camps when they're a bit older than that, and pay through the nose to do so.

Again, this wouldn't be so much of an issue if we didn't make such a fuss about the impostor, triumph. We are now fifth in the medals table, having leapfrogged France, but then been leapfrogged by them again, which means that we are at this point the fifth best country in the world at everything. The best country in the world is China. The USA and South Korea are also better than us, but we are still, astonishingly, better than Russia, who languish in tenth, perhaps because Mikhail Gorbachev dismantled their private education system in 1989.

In other news: Nessie has been discovered, if an unassuming bump in the water is what we mean by 'Nessie'.

BORING

4 August 2012

DAY 8

....

Women's épée

....

Well, I suppose if I am going to experience what many Londoners are going to experience during this festival, it will involve a visit to an Olympic sporting event dictated entirely by the powers of chance rather than my own preferences. In the run-up to the Games, all the talk was of the impossibility of finding tickets, of the enormous mark-ups touts would be charging, even the legitimate ones, but in the end I got them through the normal, off-hand way that so many of them have changed hands: I asked around, and sure enough, a friend of a friend came up with one ticket to the quarter-finals of the women's épée, and another with two to the semi-finals of the women's beach volleyball, which I will be attending tomorrow, and all costing me no more than the price printed on the ticket itself.

In one respect, though, I am already skewing the results of the experiment by participating in it. Under normal circumstances, i.e. without being contracted to write about the subject, I would no more think of going to one of the events than I would of taking my summer holidays in Syria. And not only do I have to fight through my own reluctance to get there, I have to do so at stupid o'clock on a Saturday morning, a time usually reserved for long sleep followed by leisurely repose with the *Guardian*. For the ticket says '9 a.m.' on it, and I live some way away from East London, and some rubric I recall seeing somewhere told me to get to the venue an hour and a half before the event starts. Well, bollocks to that, I'm not getting there at 7.30, but I still have a distressingly early start.

East London has always both fascinated and repelled me, rather as I suppose the residents of Middle Earth might have been fascinated and repelled by Mordor. It also appears to be equally hard to get to. ('My dear Frodo, one does not simply walk into Canning Town.') The event is being held in the ExCeL Centre, a venue I have always avoided on the grounds that I never have anything to do with words with capital letters in the middle of them, and also that it looks like the millennium dome's ill-favoured younger brother, just a big, heartless cuboid squatting like a lump by the side of the river. (Looking to see if there's anything interesting about it I can pinch off Wikipedia, I notice that Wikipedia itself loses patience with the entry by the time it gets to the paragraph titled 'Corporate Social Responsibility': 'This article appears to be written like an advertisement,' it sighs, next to the warning sign of a large exclamation mark, the kind that old-school newspapermen call 'a screamer'. 'Please help improve it by rewriting promotional content from a neutral point of view and removing any inappropriate external links.' Do so, please, and if you manage to squeeze in a quote from me I'll buy you a drink.)

Searching the Transport for London website for tips on how to get there, I redirect myself, at their instigation, to LOCOG's suggested route for 2012 spectators. This site seems to have a few bugs in it, and I am told to go by some crazy route involving a tram and a bus which would appear to have a letter in its name (always the leper-bell for the person reluctant to leave central London), which will take me an hour and seven minutes. Intuition tells me that this can't be right, and indeed TfL themselves suggest a much quicker route that will take me about half an hour, involving the Docklands Light Railway. Which pleases me, for I remember that because the trains are driverless, you can sit at the front and watch the rails coming towards you. This is old hat for New Yorkers, but for Londoners who live further west than the DLR, this is a big deal, and more than makes up for the uncomfortable feeling – part guilt, part future shock – I get when boarding a train without a human at the helm.

This is my first exposure to the Games in real life. The last week and a bit have been spent no further from the TV than the shop over the road to buy tobacco and the Majestic Wine a little bit further down to buy booze. Interactions with London during the Games have, as per the Mayor's suggestion that I lay off the public transport, been confined to hearing the whistles of the police motorbikes as they stop the cross-traffic from tangling itself up with the Olympic lane on Gloucester Place and Baker Street (the sign that went up a few weeks ago telling people to stay out of the lane now says 'all traffic use Olympic lanes'. Tchoh! One minute they're telling us to keep out of the lane, now they're saying it's the only one we can use). On the way there, the tube fills up with people wearing OCOG (*sic*) Games passes round their necks; their names and job titles are displayed prominently. R— H—, who might benefit from laying off the McDonald's for a while, is, I learn, one of the officers on the 'Handball team liaison team'. I also see my first man with a gloriously distended belly wearing a 'Team GB' shirt.

Still, it is a pleasure to use the DLR, which goes up and down too, like a slightly flattened funfair ride, even if it's only for one stop, and when I get off at the designated station, some fifteen minutes' walk from the ExCeL Centre, I am pointed, about every twenty paces or so, by smiling volunteers in the pink and purple LOCOG uniforms with giant foam hands, in the direction I'm meant to be going. A group of people as diverse in age and race as you could wish for, they look happy to be doing their work, however unpaid, and their good humour is infectious. It's bright and breezy outside, and East London feels, as it always does to me, as though I've landed in a foreign country: but one where, miraculously, you can understand every word of the local argot, and with only a minimal inflection to my own speech (I twist the dial on the back of my neck to 'Mockney lite') I can even pass off as one of the natives.

I have already noticed the cable car from the train. And there it is again: yet another New Thing in London, impossibly high, majestic almost, a place removed from earthly care. That's what I want, I think to myself: elevation. Elevation. Let's get a bit of perspective on this, and find out if we can even see another land.

But all too soon I am at the ExCeL Centre, having passed through housing estates that look as though they're no more than a year old, past people walking their dogs by the river ('Those are Canada Geese,' explains one woman to her dog, a massive brute which seems torn as to whether the geese or I would make the tastier breakfast), the now ornamental cranes lining the dead wharves, reminding us what used to be here, once. This area might look young, but it feels old, old, and that East London atmosphere will never go away as long as it remains the mouth of London (whereas I live in its gut). Old and young at once: it makes me think of those children you sometimes see, with shockingly wise and knowing faces, that unsettlingly make you think of reincarnation.

After a little banter at the x-ray machines and metal detectors, where you even have to take off your belt ('Have anyone's trousers fallen down yet?', 'I've been here three days, and I'm still waiting'), I make it into the stadium, and am disconcerted to see stalls selling food other than McDonald's and drinks other than Heineken and Coke, which blows one of my pet peeves about the Games out of the water. On approaching the entrance to my stand, I am told that the quarter-final does not start until 10.30, that 9 a.m. on my ticket was when they wanted me to get there, not when they started clashing swords. Well, I have my book, and my paper, and fleeing Spandau Ballet's 'Gold' being blasted from the speakers because it is the toxic yuppie anthem, followed by Roxy Music's 'Avalon', which reminds me of a painful love affair from thirty years ago, I go for a wander and buy a surprisingly good bacon roll while keeping an eye on the spectators as they arrive: afro wigs in comedy flag colours, a group of men with the French *tricouleur* painted on their hair (the central white stripe unfortunately recalling the amorous cartoon skunk Pépé le Pew), young women in stars-and-stripes leggings who have painted 'USA' on their cheeks and even their lips painted in rough approximations of Old Glory. ('Where are you from?' I feel like asking, until I ungenerously decide that maybe the joke might be lost on them, and they'd just think I was stupid.) A poster with a picture of a bluebell-carpeted wood has the caption 'Discover the untouched beauty of Britain's ancient woodland', and although I have read my Oliver Rackham – you must, too – and know that there is no such thing as untouched woodland in this country, I suffer a powerful pang to escape to the countryside. I notice, too, that there are a few payphones lining the walls, and that little strips of silver gaffer tape have been placed over the manufacturer's name, so I peel one off right under the eyes of an unbothered LOCOG volunteer, and can here reveal that they are made by Solitaire 6000 Payphones, should you ever feel like installing one in your own home yourself. I also note that we are urged by Coca-Cola to recycle our bottles here, because if we do so it will make us 'feel like a winner', although I do not recall any actual winners, on being asked how they feel, replying 'as good as someone who has put an empty bottle of Coke in a recycling bin'.

There are a few boards giving us glimpses of the history of fencing as an Olympic sport: I appreciate the picture of the Russian fencer Tatiana Logounova, striking at her opponent, extraordinarily, with her arm curling behind her head (so as not to transgress the piste; this move helped her win gold in 2004), and the fencing masks and swords from the turn of the twentieth century, which look very similar to the kit I wore during my brief flirtation with the sport when I was about twelve, in the bit-later-than-mid-twentieth century.

And so, with half an hour to go, to my seat; a military brass band, wearing what looks exactly like Corporal Jones's dress uniform from the Zulu campaign, run smartly through such classics as 'It's Not Unusual'. Screens tell us that a Chinese athlete called Dong Dong has won the trampoline event, and a young MC with a microphone and his own personal cameraman warms up the crowd by getting us all to cheer and drum our feet. I do not do so, but I smile indulgently, in case the cameras capture me. We are given some primer lessons on the art and scoring systems of fencing. I think I gave up fencing because they said I was too young for the sabre, but that was the only one I craved, for you could slash with it as well as stab, and it had a hand guard that went round the whole hand, like a proper sword, as used by the three musketeers.

Then the fencers come in, in procession, to the strains of 'London Calling' (without the vocals). Our gazes switch from the screens to the athletes. I must say, this is rather impressive. Without their helmets, they look stern, serious, disciplined. Gorgeously so, if I may put it like that. And even in this marginal sport, it is hard not to get caught up in the excitement; it is, in fact, highly dramatic, and even though I understand it is ironic that they are being accompanied by the music for a punk classic whose first release I am old enough to remember, and which imagines an apocalyptic scenario, my mind can't really process this irony, and instead I thrill to the noise, the celebration of physical perfection and the nobility of the sport. I feel fear: this is how fascism starts.

Thankfully, the sport itself is really boring to watch, or certainly more fun to engage in than to watch, for the uninitiated. In this I suppose it's rather like cricket, a comparison which might have been suggested by the white clothing. Tick, tickety, zing, tick, go the clashing swords – when they do clash, that is. It comes back to me that fencing, like chess, is one of those sports where an aggressive move makes you also immediately vulnerable to counter-aggression, so much time is spent bouncing up and down on the balls of your feet, the tip of the sword making little circles, waiting for the other fencer to blink, so to speak: or, as the technical jargon has it, dicking around. (The American one has the stars and stripes painted on the mesh of her mask; does this intimidate her opponents, or galvanize them, I wonder?)

The woman in front of me, who has turned up with three children and presumably her husband, looks round and asks me if I know anything about fencing. When the light on their helmet goes on, does that mean they've been hit, or that they have hit? And that score, asks the child next to her, is a lower score better or a higher one? I give my answers to these questions to the best of my knowledge, along with a theatrically self-deprecating 'I think', but as the matches progress I begin to get a horrible suspicion that I have given exactly the wrong replies, and so it is not only boredom that propels me from my seat after a mere hour, but embarrassment. After being given directions to the way out by a couple of good-natured squaddies and a couple of equally good-natured LOCOG volunteers,* I go to the Emirates cable car and have the most memorable time, for I discover that it is not so much vertigo I suffer from as a very specific fear of being in a cable car 300 hundred feet above the ground, and that car detaching itself from its cable and plunging to earth with nothing you can do about it except scream and commend your soul to God. Which I think you will agree rather beats the thrill of sport, even watching serious-looking women carrying *swords*.

Later on this evening, as I lay down my pen after writing the above, I check on the medals table and see that Great Britain is now in third place. We are now a better, more moral country than South Korea, but America and China are still better and more moral countries than us. Yet I cannot help a little flash of pride, like a goldfish's fin, in the murky pond that passes for my soul.

---

* And here is another confounding thing: not only is the volunteers' good cheer clearly unfeigned, and, as I have said, infectious, there is also plenty of evidence that the squaddies and the civvies are getting on nicely. I also notice that there are many of that demographic under-represented in the media, the – let's not mince our words – middle-aged woman. If I may speculate, these women with the momentum of years of under-appreciated domestic industry under their belt and time on their hands, the children having flown the nest, still feel they have energy left and great reserves of generosity, and have thought: well, I've been doing stuff without pay for years, I know how to help people who need guidance, I have a bit of time on my hands, this kind of thing doesn't happen very often – so why not help out? It is certainly shameful that cleaners at the sites are being paid very little, are accommodated in shitholes and have to pay for their accommodation on top of everything else. But at least, here, something is going right.

5 August 2012

DAY 9

··

Women's Boxing
Men's Singles Tennis
Women's Beach Volleyball

··

First, the women's boxing: or, as they call it in some of America, 'Foxy Boxing'. Which should at once alert us to part of the problem. Natasha Jones, the Briton, triumphs over the American, Quanitta Underwood, after having delivered what the commentator describes as some 'very hurtful punches'.

I think it might be said that if you have a problem with women boxing, then you probably have, without knowing it, a problem with boxing. One problem I have is that writers are meant to like boxing: or, at least, there are plenty who claim to. This makes me suspicious. It's pretty much the opposite of what they do, and they like to show people that they are not the milquetoasts that the general public assumes them to be, that they are men of the world, with the common touch, open to extreme experience. Vladimir Nabokov, before giving a name-check of the usual suspects, wrote this:

'What matters, of course, is not really that a heavyweight boxer is a little bloodied after two or three rounds, or that the white vest of the referee looks as though red ink has leaked out of a fountain pen. What matters is, first, the beauty of the art of boxing, the perfect accuracy of the lunges, the side jumps, the dives, the range of blows – hooks, straights, swipes – and, secondly, the wonderful manly excitement which this art arouses' (translation by Anastasia Tolstoy and Thomas Karshan).

Now, Nabokov rather famously never used a word without deliberation, and while he didn't write this in English there is no reason to suppose the translators have got it wrong. So when we have the words 'manly excitement' and 'arouses' coming close together in the same sentence, we have to acknowledge that Nabokov may be thinking about something more than aesthetics.

Fine. And if you think that watching two half-naked men beating the crap out of each other is a turn-on, then you are not alone. I don't, but I wouldn't say this makes me any more virtuous than those who do. After all, watching *completely* naked men beating the crap out of each other, while slathered in olive oil to boot, is what the games were all about in the first place. (The 'gymn' in 'gymnastics' means 'naked'. So when you swoon to Satie's *Gymnopédies* you are swooning to a piece of music whose name means 'naked children' – as Satie well knew.) Nabokov ends by talking about the 'beautiful feeling' that lingered in the crowd, post-match, 'a feeling of dauntless, flaring strength, vitality, manliness, inspired by the play in boxing'.

That word again, 'manly', making a slightly modified

reappearance. So what do we think when we see two women waling on each other? We have to rule out 'manly' and its cognates, don't we? 'Foxy Boxing' is a clue as to how certain men are expected to think, but all I take from the Lightweight Women's Boxing is that here we have two women throwing punches or dodging them, as opposed to two men throwing punches and dodging them, and if the bout I saw had less of the post-pub grapple about it than the judo did, it didn't look as if it would inspire anyone to the same levels of rapture that Nabokov claimed to experience when he saw a match, and, if anything, might give rise to the suspicion that when writers go into spasms of delight when describing boxing, it is in some part a matter of covering up for either preferences, or inadequacies, which they would prefer not to address directly, and so therefore can be filed under the category of Self-Deluding Bullshit, or, to put it more charitably, the Pull of the Void, as when a very intelligent person becomes besotted by someone who is very beautiful but also very stupid.

Here is a good pub quiz question: which sport has been in every modern Olympics, apart from Stockholm in 1920, because it was illegal? Boxing, of course. The sport was banned in Sweden until 2007, which I suppose is one way of dating the precise year when the Enlightenment project failed altogether. Professional boxing is the most dangerous sport there is, and the repeated blows to the head lead almost inevitably to some kind of damage. There is a poignant phrase used by doctors to describe the kind of thing that happens inside your head when the outside is repeatedly and violently pummelled: 'an insult to the brain'.

★

In the men's tennis, Andy Murray is, as they say in the news media, exorcising some Wimbledon ghosts, by, as they don't say in the news media, handing Roger Federer's arse to him on a plate. (As I write, Murray leads Federer 4–2 in the third set, having won the first two sets 6–2, 6–1. Were this a real tennis match, i.e. Wimbledon proper, this would now be the time for Murray to crumble and Federer to turn things around and win the match after all.)

But as you all know, Murray claimed the gold, even though Federer came off the court with the easy gait of someone who has, out of camaraderie, the goodness of his heart, and because he knows how much it means to the other guy, let his opponent win. And if you think this is a slur on Murray's victory, you have to admit that Federer certainly did not even begin to look anything like as crushed at the Olympic final as Murray did after the Wimbledon one.

Murray, after recovering from the shock, looks happy, though – as he has every right to be – dancing across the court after climbing up the stands to hug friends, coaches and family (as well as, touchingly, one small boy, whose relationship, if any, to Murray is uncommented on), he drapes himself in the Union Jack to defuse the perennial debate as to whether his loyalties lie with that flag or the Saltire, and the question about the relative significance of an Olympic Gold and a Grand Slam title is unasked. Do you know who won Olympic Gold in Athens, 2004? That we all know who has won in 2012 doesn't mean that the tournament itself has somehow mysteriously *grown up*, but that Murray is now, post-Wimbledon, subject to an even greater level of scrutiny than hitherto, and besides, we're staring obsessively at every event, because this is our showcase, and validates any excuse to relieve the however-many-years-of-hurt it is since we last won X (much was made of the fact that our gymnastic bronze in 2012 was our first medal in the discipline for a hundred years). It's a consolation prize, that's all. A good one, but not the Real Thing; it's a big chocolate coin of a medal (for some reason, photographers have encouraged winners to bite the medals, as if to test their purity, even though we know they're only 6 per cent gold), and not the rather more substantial Wimbledon trophy.

As you can see, this Sunday finds me in something of a grump, so I hope to cheer myself up by going along to Horse Guard's Parade to see one of the quarter-finals of the Women's Beach Volleyball – which in this case is USA versus the Czech Republic (landlocked, as I recall, so with little in the way of beach to practise. Plucky Czech Republic for getting so far!). This is, it goes without saying, the acceptable face of mass public voyeurism. (The women pole vaulters' outfits, to take one example, are no less revealing than the beach volley-ballers', yet they do not attract anything like the same level of lecherous attention.) Boris Johnson can go on about the competitors glistening like 'wet otters' ('wet as an otter's pocket' is a simile used to describe the vagina of a woman in a state of great sexual arousal, and it is unimaginable that Johnson does not know this, and is not consciously referencing it. We got the reference, anyway, all right) without attracting too much censure, as always.

The event I have tickets for starts at ten o'clock at night, which when I first see it I fear is a misprint, but no, at least

LOCOG's pre-games incompetence does not extend to its proofreading. The late start is, I suspect (as with the opening ceremony's), a gesture towards the American market, so, in the eastern time zone at least, they can watch it without cutting into the working day. Not that anyone in the audience appears to mind: everyone seems pretty tanked up, even more than I am (I thought it best to have a glass or two beforehand, so that my mood was not too out of kilter with everyone else's); it is a warm and pleasant night, we're in the middle of town and not in the boondocks of the Olympic Park, and no one really gives a flying one who wins as long as there is lots of toned female skin on display.

In this, the Czech team could be said to have fallen at the first hurdle, for they are wearing black track suits. While at least not loose-fitting, these do not offer much to the lubricious gaze of the crowd. The Americans are in bikini bottoms, though not in bikini tops; and anyway, my seat is as far away from the action as it is possible to get,* so I watch the event as pure sport without being distracted by any other considerations.

Well, *qua* sport, we are working at a rudimentary level here. The rules can be explained and picked up in about two seconds, which presumably is the whole point. This isn't about sport, it's about a fun night out, and the atmosphere is part holiday camp singalong, part late-night baseball

---

* In being placed right at the back of the stands, I discover I possess another, very specific, phobia: of being knocked over the rear wall in a freak accident and plummeting to my death a long, long way below. It happens: it's how Ned Flanders's wife met her end in *The Simpsons*.

match, part pissed-up rally and part stag party. We are at the centre of power in the land, and the warm-up MC names each side of the arena after the street that runs along behind it. 'David Cameron wants to get an early night!' he yells. 'No chance! Go Downing Street!' I am in Downing Street, so I give a cheer, too.

And then . . . well, I had been wondering whether the rise of beach volleyball had anything to do with the pornification of society, and although there is something in that – the cheerleaders who bump and grind between sets (I say 'between sets' but they seem to come on at arbitrary intervals) might as well be so many porn stars – what the spectacle really represents is the stupidification of society. If watching the sport on TV gave you the impression that there were at least trace elements of the Corinthian ideal in it, that this is a sport which does not cry out to have inverted commas around the word, then watching it live will swiftly disabuse you. The only way this sport could be made less serious would be if people were made to play it in clown suits, or naked, or with balloons (it recalls those anaphrodisiac little films about nudist camps which showed people in the nip pushing a ball back and forth over a net). In the crowd, people here and there boo the US team in a way which would be unimaginable, or heavily frowned upon, at any other Olympic event. I feel like asking why they're booing the Americans, but the otherwise jolly white thirty-somethings who are doing so might take umbrage with me for asking them, and I decide to be English about this and do nothing, except brood, and wonder what de Coubertin would have made of this event.

As it is, the Czechs give the Americans a run for their money in the first game (first to 21, but a 2-point lead necessary), but they collapse a bit in the second, I think. I say 'I think' because the Mexican waves are going perpetually round the ground during the action. There's thumping rock music between each point, the screen flashes the words 'POWERFUL SPIKE!', 'AMAZING' and 'SPECTACULAR' every so often. Are those last two technical terms? For all the pedigree and dignity of the game, they may be. And yes, they do play 'Yakkedy Yak', the *Benny Hill Show* theme tune, whenever the players leave the pitch and the men come on to rake the sand.

Of course, the atmosphere is good-humoured. How could it fail to be? I can't bring this lot down all by myself. Waiting for a pee, I hear the man behind me marvel at the fact that this is the first public event he's ever been to where the queues for the men's loos are far longer than those for the women's. I say to him that perhaps it's because rather more men than women applied for tickets, and that gets a laugh. An Englishman a few people down the line in front of me is speaking to a man behind him. 'You Brazilian mate? Yeah? Loads of sexy ladies in Brazil, know what I mean?' Actually, scratch what I said about this having the atmosphere of a stag party – it's got the atmosphere of a lap-dancing club.

It's about this time of the evening that the phrase I had remembered about boxing injuries pops up in my head – the 'insult to the brain'. Well, here's another one. Sadly, I reflect that my attitude towards this event does not show great consistency. If I'm not as impressed by sport as everyone says I should be, why should I be bothered by this? I am like one of the *kvetchers* in the restaurant: 'The food here is lousy.' 'Yes, and such small portions.' Well, there you go. I *kvetch*.

On the way out, as I exit with the chimes of Big Ben (from what we must now, post-Jubilee, call the Elizabeth Tower) rolling and echoing mightily off the walls of the Foreign and Commonwealth Office and HM Treasury and Cabinet Office in King Charles Street, a very drunk woman leaving behind me demands to be given a thorough frisking from a squaddie on duty at the gates, which shows that at least she's got into the spirit of the evening.

Zoe Williams, at the end of an article in the *Guardian* praising women's boxing in general and the bout between Natasha Jones and Quanitta Underwood in particular, writes: 'I would still prefer it if people didn't hit one another, and I would prefer it, just for this one fight, if both people could have won . . .'

In other news: a white man shoots six dead at a Sikh temple in Wisconsin, before being shot and then killing himself.

6 August 2012

DAY 10

....

Men's 100m (aftermath)
More Horses
Cycling

....

Usain Bolt's victory is all over the papers this morning: the
Guardian dispenses with all copy on its front page to celebrate the Jamaican's victory. Inside, we are told that he will
earn £21 million from Puma alone in endorsement deals,
which is, in effect, a salary of over £2 million a second.
Shortly before he ran the race, though, a man threw an
empty plastic beer bottle onto the track. Unfortunately for
him, he was standing next to a Dutch judoka (although it
would appear that the judoka's skills were not deployed).
He was charged, pleonastically, with 'intending to cause
intentional harassment, alarm or distress', and we await his
fate. Whether his action was prompted by some kind of mental disturbance or something more political remains to be
seen. Along with the man who sent Tom Daley a couple of
unpleasant texts (and, when this book comes out, me and

Mr Shrigley) the wrath of a state which has seen the Olympic Spirit, or the fun and games, traduced, is looking at the most barbaric treatment available in law. (I will be going into hiding for a few months until this all blows over.) Even Charlie Brooker, the reliably curmudgeonly *Guardian* columnist, for whom I entertain no little respect, is enjoying himself. The whole country is getting into line, and criticism will not be tolerated.

So what are they going to do with Sir Keith Mills, who was chief executive of the London bid and is now deputy chair of the organizing committee? He has warned that unless £1bn of resources are diverted to encouraging sport at a national level, 'things will go back to how they were. It will be like a Chinese meal – we'll have a big blowout in the summer and go back to feeling hungry in three months' time.'

Leaving aside the rather old-school remarks about Chinese food, he has a point, although his proposal is for a nightmare future where we are not going to be able to divert ourselves with anything apart from the various sports we have been doing rather well in so far. There is not an infinite ocean of money to spend on this, *after all*; and I wonder whether there will be an infinite ocean of public affection for it, either. We have already spent rather a lot on these Games, even allowing for all the cost-cutting that's been going on where it has been thought we can get away with it – namely, in the number of volunteers that have been giving their time for free, and the way minimum-wage cleaners have been obliged to pay for their own wretched accommodation. And the sponsors, who have garnered perhaps more than 12 per cent of the publicity despite paying for only about 12 per cent of the Games, will not consider a running track in Lichfield as tasty a venue as one being visited by thousands of people from around the world. We have also been told that 40,000 jobs have been created as a result of these games: but how many of them will still be there when they pack up for Rio?

It is all going to come down to that word again: legacy. This is going to be a word we will hear being raised with increasing petulance, and maybe even irony, over the forthcoming months, maybe years. What is, I wonder, the legacy of Usain Bolt going to be? It will make the people of Jamaica very happy. It's made pretty much everyone happy – everyone loves the Jamaicans (apart from people in the neighbouring isles of the West Indies, of course). But then?

In 1944 George Orwell reviewed *A Letter to My Son*, a short book by Osbert Sitwell, which championed the cause of the independent, free-thinking artist, from a lofty perspective. Orwell said it was 'sometimes unfair and occasionally frivolous', but largely approved. Three months later, he noticed a counter-blast by James Agate, in his day a very well-known diarist and theatre critic, which said, among other things, that various sports have 'moved the ordinary man more than all the poets put together'.

This is part of a timeless debate, although it's one that isn't aired too often these days, largely because either High Art has retreated, or even given up, in terror of being called elitist,* or because 'the Arts' are now simply subsumed into the

---

* The gift shop at the Royal Opera House has had all its stock replaced and has been turned into an Olympic Shop – Wenlocks, proud only to accept Visa, etc. – *until the middle of September.*

same gaudy, happy feel-good tent where we can forget our troubles for a while. But it was alive in 1944, as a nation began to think about what was going to happen after the war.

Orwell replied to Agate and nailed the debate by pointing out that sport's achievements are ephemeral. 'Shakespeare has made life more worth living for ten generations of Englishmen, while W. G. Grace, even granting that his famous stroke which broke the clock in the Lord's pavilion was somehow the equivalent of *Macbeth* or *King Lear*, is already a fading memory.' How true; and even the sporting moments which I cherish – Graham Gooch's 333 at Lord's against India, Arsenal's last-gasp winner in the 1979 FA Cup final, etc., etc. – are *over*, by definition never to be repeated, and, ultimately, capable of saying nothing; whereas anyone can pick up an edition of *The Waste Land* and not only feel its intensity anew again and again, but often come away with more to think about than they did before. This is not to complain about sport: this is its purpose, but in recognizing that we shouldn't inflate its worth or significance into a shape it is unable to maintain. 'I have made a monument more lasting than bronze,' wrote Horace immodestly but accurately, about his own art, 2,000 years ago; and more lasting than silver, or gold, too.*

★

* The last word was, as was so often the case, Orwell's, as he reflected on the famous bad taste of the British public. You might think that this has nothing to do with the subject of this book, but 'bad taste' has been a feature of the London Olympics ever since, to a collective gasp of disbelief, its appalling logo was unveiled, and then the typeface, and then the purple-and-pink uniforms of the volunteers . . . and then it occurred to me

Later on, the BBC shows a long clip of children being interviewed about how excited they are about the Olympics.
'Inspire a generation' goes the slogan: and it is nice for children to be thrilled by the events – although when I was nine,
Mark Spitz's remarkable achievements at the Olympics
didn't exactly inspire me to become a champion swimmer –
although they certainly made me hate and fear the swimming
pool a lot less, and I may have even entertained some enthu-
siasm for it, for a while. Another inspiration, more troubling
in retrospect, was his moustache: I thought it would be really
cool to grow one. My point is not entirely flippant. Children
are fertile ground for the seeds of inspiration, but the flowers
are fragile, easily uprooted and often supplanted by other,
less gaudy growths. It is also true that there are things people
can be which they do not realize are desirable when they are
young: artists, poets, novelists, software engineers, songwrit-
ers, entrepreneurs, inventors, mechanics, accountants, and
on and on ... but it is remarkable how a VT montage of

---

that whatever the opening ceremony was, however much fun it was, or
so satisfyingly incomprehensible to foreigners, you couldn't say it was
tasteful. So here's more Orwell: 'We in this country have bad taste, as we
have bad teeth, because of complex but discoverable social causes. It is a
thing to be fought against ... The artist fights it by preserving his integ-
rity: the critic fights against it by educating the public. And flattery is not
a form of education. [There has been a great deal of *flattery* in these
Olympics, hasn't there? After the pre-Games griping, we're now flattering
ourselves for just about everything to do with them ...] To assume that the
big public is inevitably composed of fools, and then to imply that there is
something lovable and even meritorious in being a fool, is less useful and
less admirable than retreating to an ivory tower with all the windows
barred.'

children saying what they'd like to do when they grow up (as long as that profession fits the flavour of the moment; in this case, 'sport') is a way of short-circuiting all criticism, thought and rational enquiry. And, while we're at it, let's not forget the hypocrisy of complaining about the Chinese for sending their children off to sport camps when what we are trying to do is encourage children to do something similar. An athlete, though, is a useful person to have for a government anxious to distract attention from the disastrous way it is managing a country. Athletes are not there to think, or to observe, or to cast doubt.

Nick Skelton, the 54-year-old equestrian, in his sixth Olympics, has won, along with the rest of his team, a gold medal in more horsey riding. Three things: 1. He does not sound posh. 2. When you hear how many of his team-mates and fellow riders, including him, have broken their necks over the years and still got back on their horseys, you have to salute their dedication. And 3. I really, really like the idea of an Olympian older than I am. (Who also, unlike the even older Japanese equestrian, Hiroshi Hoketsu, looks properly his age.)

'Kenny is literally on fire.' No, he's not. (He's a jolly good bicycle rider, but he is very clearly aware of the ins and outs of maintaining a flame-proof bike and kit. He's not even *smoking*.)*

* Pointing out occasions when 'literally' has been used in the sense of 'figuratively' has long been a staple of snooty commentary, and I think the time is coming when there's simply going to be nothing to gain any more

Velodrome: nice that we keep that name, in honour of the way the French are traditionally held to own the sport of cycling; but then we used to own football, cricket and about half the sports being played at the Olympics. Over the years, we have learned to give them away, more or less gracefully, with more or less dignity, and it is in a way disconcerting to be claiming some of them back – somehow *un-British*. I wonder if this is happening all too fast, and we will suffer some kind of psychic damage as a result. This is not exactly what Sir Keith Mills is worrying about, I think, but the mood in the country is going to be decidedly odd for a while afterwards, like that of a boy at a party who managed to snog the prettiest girl and can't quite believe, the next day, that he did it at all.

In the quarter-finals of the sprint, Victoria Pendleton makes the competitor from Belarus, in a two-man race, look as though she's actually *stopped*, she overtakes her so fast. Again, despite myself, I am impressed.

Watching one of the semi-finals in the women's football, I see the Americans on their way to a 4–3 victory over the Canadians. The level of skill shown is, to this admittedly non-expert eye, unimpressive. In fact, if it seems unimpressive

---

by mentioning when it happens. Language evolves, we know, and I have given up public utterance on complaining about 'hopefully' being misused, and I still wince when people say 'I'm good' when they mean 'I'm fine', but hold my tongue; but it is still a sad day when a word like 'literally' literally ceases to have any link to its real meaning any more.

to my eye, it must be either unwatchable or comically compelling for an expert.

The 400m hurdles, we are told, is known as 'the man killer'.
My housemate, uncharacteristically drunk after a succession
of hot toddies she has been treating her flu with, tweets that,
funnily enough, her vagina is known as the 400m hurdles,
and gains about 3,000 followers as a result.

In other news: Nick Clegg, a young politician in the UK's
coalition government, has announced that he is fed up with
the Tories, and we are reminded that even when the best
intentions and the highest hopes attend the commencement
of an enterprise, it can have its rocky patches, and even end
in disaster.

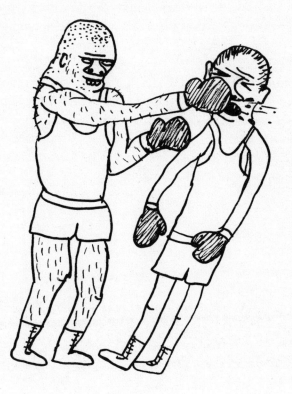

7 August 2012

DAY 11

....

The Discus

....

I am beginning to think that maybe the nation is gorging on
spectacle and is feeling a little queasy. The satirical on-line
magazine the *Daily Mash* pre-emptively suggested this
yesterday in an article whose headline was 'Nation's
Euphoria Gone By Midday'. It went on to say that 'a combination of commuting and re-acquaintance with work
colleagues means that by the time the country consumes its
sad vacuum-packed sandwiches at its collective desks, the
Olympics will once more be that thing in London that cost
too much.'

And that ambiguous national treasure, Morrissey, has
entered the debate by writing on his website:

I am unable to watch the Olympics due to the blustering
jingoism that drenches the event. Has England ever been quite
so foul with patriotism?

The 'dazzling royals' have, quite naturally, hi-jacked the Olympics for their own empirical needs, and no oppositional voice is allowed in the free press. It is lethal to witness.

As London is suddenly promoted as a super-wealth brand, the England outside London shivers beneath cutbacks, tight circumstances and economic disasters. Meanwhile the British media present 24-hour coverage of the 'dazzling royals', laughing as they lavishly spend, as if such coverage is certain to make British society feel fully whole.

In 2012, the British public is evidently assumed to be undersized pigmies, scarcely able to formulate thought.

This from a man who has flirted with, or at least engaged with, far-right politics (his 'National Front Disco' I consider one of the most fascinating and dangerously complex treatments of the subject I can recall), and literally – yes, literally – covered himself in the Union Jack in his 1992 Finsbury Park concert. Famously a man of contradictions, and with a long history of putting his foot in his mouth or at least antagonizing an enormous number of people with practically every utterance, he nevertheless remains an almost officially countenanced conduit of dissidence against the prevailing consensus – perhaps because he rarely does his cause any favours by expressing himself the way he so often does. (Is an undersized 'pigmy' [*sic*] just a pygmy, or an especially small pygmy? And what is an 'empirical' need? Did he mean to say 'imperial'?)

But, in case I thought he was protesting too much, here's this from the *Daily Mail*'s website today, written by Conservative MEP Daniel Hannan:

The Olympic Games have brought British patriotism back into fashion: British patriotism in its broadest, most benevolent, most generous form.

Watching the first event, the men's cycling road race, in Surrey, I sensed that something had changed.

Every house along the route was draped with Union flags. The people in front of those houses were cheerfully handing round drinks and sandwiches to strangers, united by the warm feeling that they were all hoping for the same thing . . .

and so on. You get the idea, and if a Tory is gladdened by the sight of so many Union Jacks in the streets, then we need neither be surprised nor affronted. It is the nature of things. Keeping to the script, he also makes a point that it is bad news for proponents of devolution. But then he strays into very political territory indeed:

. . . the sight of so many delirious parents watching their now grown-up children – the children whom they had happily ferried to training session after training session – is a reminder that families are much better than government agencies as providers of education, inspiration, healthcare, social security and discipline.

. . . the Games are a vindication of competition in schools. Some Leftie columnists have been whining about the fact that a disproportionate number of the athletes were educated in the independent sector, but what does this tell us?

The answer is that, in general, independent schools have encouraged competitive sports in the realization that the

flawed 'all must have prizes' philosophy is a poor preparation
for life beyond the school gates.

Well, to answer the main points made, there must be very
few people aside from – let me try to be neutral about this,
and use a different adjective from the one I originally used –
the most committed libertarian anti-statist who would really
argue that families are better than schools or hospitals or
unemployment benefit or the police at their jobs. Indeed the
comparison is effectively without meaning. And all the disproportionate number of independent schools represented
in the British medal tables tells us is that they have, as I and
many others have already pointed out, far superior resources.

The problem is not so much that this is drivel, overheated
by circumstance and the sheer rush-of-blood-to-head giddi-
ness of rhetoric that the *Daily Mail* encourages (Hannan
does not have a reputation as a *particularly* thoughtless
blowhard), but that the Games are being used as a peg, as
an excuse for every jumped-up commentator to get on his
hind legs and see only what he wants to see.

But it does raise one interesting question that has to be
both contemplated and addressed by the left: how to react
to the Games. Or, to put it another way, how to claim them.
As things stand at the moment, the honours are about even,
insofar as the general reaction has been to stand by the flag.
On one level, though, they're a disaster for the left, and especially the cynical, *Guardian*-reading left, of which it will
probably by now come as no surprise to you to learn I count
myself a member (Team Lefty Whiner, so to speak). So I do
a little thought experiment: what would I be saying now if

Team GB* had had a much scanter tally of trophies than they have as I write, or the organization of the Games had descended into the kind of farce that Mitt Romney was so desperate to warn us and the rest of the world about. I would decry the waste of money, the hubris before the event, and a whole lot of other I-told-you-so stuff, and this book would consist of a long catalogue of humiliation and incompetence.

But as it is, so far – I don't want to tempt fate – it is all going rather well, and if you thought I was going to include myself modestly among the list of jumped-up commentators who see only what they want to, you'd be wrong, for I'm seeing lots of stuff I didn't want to see, or certainly wasn't expecting to, and that, as far as I'm concerned, is much more interesting.

Meanwhile, the *Guardian* once again unpatriotically fails to get behind the coalition government by pointing out that it has sold another twenty school playing fields since the 2010 election, despite promises that it would do no such thing.

From today's *Guardian* website:

Seven members of the Cameroon Olympic team have disappeared during London 2012, according to the country's Ministry of Sports and Physical Education.

---

* A formulation I like no more than I did when I first heard it, which doubtless those such as Hannan would say tells its own story; but in this case it is not sniggering treachery that propels my dislike, but a wish to clasp my beloved English language to my breast and kiss away its tears.

The seven – five boxers, a swimmer and a footballer – are suspected of having left to stay in Europe for economic reasons.

The team's head, David Ojong, said: 'What began as rumour has finally turned out to be true. Seven Cameroonian athletes who participated at the 2012 London Olympic Games have disappeared from the Olympic Village.'

Ojong said a reserve goalkeeper for the women's football team, Drusille Ngako, was the first to disappear. She was not one of the 18 players retained after pre-Olympic training in Scotland, and when the team left for Coventry she vanished.

A few days later, the swimmer Paul Ekane Edingue also went missing, and on Sunday the five boxers eliminated from the Games – Thomas Essomba, Christian Donfack Adjoufack, Abdon Mewoli, Blaise Yepmou Mendouo and Serge Ambomo – also reportedly disappeared from the Olympic Village.

International Olympic Committee officials said on Tuesday they had heard nothing about the missing athletes.

Someone has smuggled what has been described as 'a bucket of unofficial condoms' into the Olympic Village. An enterprising eugenicist would have put pinholes in the lot of them. A master race of miscegenated athletes would be unbeatable, surely, although the nationalities would be contestable further down the line. Another opportunity lost.

Laura Trott wins another gold medal for Britain's cyclists, in the Omnium. She was born with a collapsed lung, I learn, at which point I begin to despair of ever finding curmudgeonly things to say about these bloody athletes. Her victory interview reveals her to be a manifestly decent person, and I am beginning to yearn for someone, a Nazi perhaps, to come across as a bounder and cad in victory. (I have been unable to track down the highly promising comment I remember from somewhere about winning silver meaning you're just the best among the losers, and fear it may be apocryphal.) And now it is Victoria Pendleton's last race; in the first heat she beats her 'nemesis', the Australian Anna Meares, by one thousandth of a second, but is then relegated because she crossed over the line (after a bit of jostling by Meares. Boo!). Then, in the second heat, Meares simply thrashes her. There are tears upon tears from both riders but more from Meares; this Olympics has been awash with them, and to be seen to be against them is to be seen to be against emotion itself.

After this Chris Hoy wins yet another gold – and, as he is already a Sir, one wonders if he will be elevated to a dukedom after this. (Hoy, incidentally, quite disproves my observation about cyclists' very faces looking aerodynamically designed; and his father, watching the race with a banner saying 'the real McHoy', himself looks, shall we say, engagingly built more for comfort than speed. Hoy Junior, I have to add, has one of those faces it is impossible to dislike: genial, open, friendly and handsome, blast him.)

And now, on a dank evening, it is the discus. This is, surely, the quintessential Olympic sport, the one refined to the point of complete irrelevance. One can understand why it might be useful for a person to be able to jump high, or run fast (my housemate's Greek friend Yiannis – I mention his nationality because I facetiously asked him if he had any particular interest in the history of the Games; he did not, and not in its present, either – watching the hurdles yesterday said, 'You know how they could make this better? Have them being chased by lions. Release the lions!' In this case, a combined sprinting/javelin event suggests itself), or swim well . . . but the discus? The hammer, in recalling the mace of knightly jousting, might have had a marginal utility in the 1204 Olympics, but even then the idea was to keep hold of the thing rather than let it go. How does a discobolist transfer his or her talents to either everyday life, or an emergency? It is certainly true that their ability could come in handy as a frisbee for pet dinosaurs, or when traversing a minefield and needing to throw something flat and circular and metallic a long way from you, but rarely does this circumstance arise. Then again, as an art-for-art's-sake kind of guy, it is precisely this type of impracticality that appeals. Which puts me in no better a position than Zoe Williams, applauding women's boxing but wishing that no one ever hit each other during it. Anyway, at least it provides one of those commentating moments that are so cherishable: 'The discus is really flying, in the air, in this Olympics tonight.' This is true: for I remember, vividly, all those times, before the modern technique was invented, around the time of the Fosbury Flop, when it was just *rolled along the ground*.

8 August 2012

DAY 12

Taking some time off from working on this crazy little book, I try to read things which have as little to do with the Olympics as possible. You'd think that would be pretty easy: the serious literature on the Olympics is thin on the ground, and I don't have many books on sport on my shelves – not even that many cricket books.

So I find my battered old four-volume Penguin edition of Orwell's essays and journalism – and, of course, pretty quickly something comes up which is relevant to the job in hand. (See Day 10.) But when wondering how best to summarize the mood of the country, I find myself thinking: hang on, this is like the Second World War. But in a good way.

Of course, I may have been conditioned to this response by my peripheral reading, but I may also have been pushed to it by a blog from Anthony Lane in the *New Yorker* a week ago. This cosmopolitan magazine for urban sophisticates, or those who aspire to that state, did well when it hired this smooth-yet-sharp-tongued product of Sherborne and Cambridge to become not only its film critic, but its explicator of all things British to an American audience that thinks

Downton Abbey a classy drama full of shrewd social observations (and so is in desperate need to be told, by someone who knows what he's talking about, that it is no such thing).

Coming towards the end of his description of a day at the Games, he writes about being on a train:

> Early-evening flooding was provided by sunlight, not rain, and, in my car [US English for 'carriage' – ed.], a sprightly chatter broke out among strangers, as we discussed the Olympic events that we had already attended and worked ourselves into a minor frenzy over those that were yet to come. It is hard to convey the unprecedented nature of this scene, for, like the rules of weightlifting, the principles that suffuse human contact on British trains are both rigid and explicit: you *can* enter into conversation with the man sitting opposite you, but only if his hair is on fire.

Allowing for the exaggeration demanded for comic effect, this is, as all Londoners know, more or less true. Actually, now I come to think of it, less true; the Beatles were breaking this convention in the opening scenes of *A Hard Day's Night* nearly half a century ago, and I've had plenty of pleasing or sometimes surreal chats with fellow-passengers over the years, but I suppose they are the exception rather than the rule. (And the Beatles were from Liverpool, of course, and they're much friendlier up North, as Southerners are always being told, aggressively, by Northerners.)

But the idea is that we are now being transformed into a city of chatterboxes, happy to turn to our fellow straphangers and swap notes about our Olympics-viewing during the day. We are a nation united in a common purpose, with a common discourse, where you know that you can turn to the person next to you and, assuming he or she is not obviously derelict or insane, converse about something you both happen to have an opinion of, even if that opinion is no more sophisticated than 'Yeah, wasn't that great?', and I have heard evidence that people have actually been having such conversations.

The thing is, I doubt it. The people who have been claiming such encounters have been newspaper or magazine columnists, and, without wishing to impugn Mr Lane's veracity in the slightest, these are people who are not afraid of giving the truth a certain spin, or colour, to prove their point. I'll believe Lane over many another writer, but in my travels through London I have seen nothing like this, yet. (The moment I do I'll let you know, promise.) I have had conversations with strangers on public transport: but the transport involved was the Emirates cable car, where you are in close confinement with a small number of people in the most novel and extraordinary piece of public infrastructure to have hit London since the Eurostar (its impact on the traveller all the more forceful because there hasn't been nearly as much fuss made about it); and I needed to gabble a bit to get over my suddenly discovered fear of cable cars, and the other passengers were similarly excited, or impressed – and even though both termini of the car abutted Olympic venues, the conversation did not touch on the Games at all, except when one girl asked her mother where the actual stadium was.

But let us assume that Londoners are suddenly talking to each other. When Londoners pull together, instead of trying to stab each other in the back, the words that most commonly come up are 'Blitz Spirit'. Now, to compare the privations suffered by Londoners during the Second World War and those being forced to stay out of Olympic lanes or eat only McDonald's in the far reaches of the city is insulting to the former; but there it is. This is a city which feels very different right now, in a completely unexpected way: its centre of gravity has shifted, its usually packed zones depopulated, that sense of national humiliation which is the abiding memory of all Britons over twenty of previous Olympic Games (the nadir being Atlanta, where, with one gold medal, we came 36th in the table, and one British athlete was spotted selling his kit on a street corner) thoroughly dissipated; and – most interestingly of all, I think – the government is, despite its best efforts, reaping no credit for this at all, and indeed even the *Daily Telegraph*, its most loyal defender, is outraged at the government's plans to abolish the two hours a week of compulsory PE that state schools are still obliged to provide. Even the notion, still gaining traction as I write, that the absurd Boris Johnson should take on the leadership of his party so as to save it from annihilation at the next election, doesn't bother me: it won't happen, because even Cameron has more dignity than Johnson, and, loathe him though I do, he is someone I would rather represent my country in a crisis than the buffoon, and I still have enough faith in my fellow-countrymen to believe that while they may elect an evil witch or warlock to govern them, they will not, in the end, elect a clown.

Look, for instance, at the way Johnson handled the riots in London – which, as we are being reminded a lot this week, happened exactly a year ago. Quite simply, he stayed away, perhaps because he was enjoying his holiday too much, or because he suspected that his particular brand is not suited to serious trouble. If he was worried that the sight of his carefully distressed hairdo framed in the gaping windows of a burnt-out shop would elicit scorn, he was right. Anyway, his tardiness ensured that this was a self-fulfilling prophecy. A fair-weather politician, then, happy to take the credit when things are going well, and not willing to accept responsibility when the shit hits the fan. When the Olympics are over, doubtless he will keep going on and on about what a success they were; unless he is wiser than that, and knows that even Londoners who are enjoying themselves immensely right now are going to find a hangover kicks in pretty quickly when they see the size of the tab.

So while it is not quite appropriate to use the war as a handle on London's mood right now, it is useful to let that experience remind us that the city is still, despite its glaring inequalities, mostly a unit, and that, though determined not to spoil the party while it is in progress – in fact, to have a really good time during it – it is quite happy to grumble about it beforehand, and then, when all the guests have gone, start looking at the cigarette burns in the curtains, the wine stains all over the carpets, the sick in the closet, the archery set bought in a crazed moment from the all-night garage, and start asking how the hell it is all going to get cleaned up once all the volunteers have gone home and the cleaners' camps have been dismantled, and there is no money to pay for any replacements.

9 August 2012

DAY 13

....

10km Open Water
BMX
Horsey Dancing (Again)

....

A moment of clarity: although this happened on 28 July, the first day of the Games proper, I only read about it today: a man watching the cycling event from the side of the road was arrested for, basically, not smiling. Here's the report, from today's *Guardian*:

> Mark Worsfold, 54, a former soldier and martial arts instructor, was arrested on 28 July for a breach of the peace shortly before the cyclists arrived in Redhouse Park, Leatherhead, where he had sat down on a wall to watch the race. Officers from Surrey police restrained and handcuffed him and took him to Reigate police station, saying his behaviour had 'caused concern'.
>
> 'The man was positioned close to a small group of protesters and based on his manner, his state of dress and his

proximity to the course, officers made an arrest to prevent a possible breach of the peace,' Surrey police said in a statement.

There are some stories that so fit one's own narrative of how the world works that one suspects one has dreamt them up, or conjured them out of the air purely by the force of one's unconscious desire, and this is one of them. Mr Worsfold has Parkinson's disease, which in his case presents itself as muscle rigidity, which includes the inability to smile. (In a detail which I could never have invented, though, the police added that 'Worsfold had had "a number of knives" in his possession, but that these turned out to be made of rubber and for use only as display items.' Whether these rubber knives were on his person or emerged after a search of his home is not made clear, but the detail adds to the trippy atmosphere that has wafted around the periphery of the Games since the opening ceremony.)

So: all shall smile, and those who do not are not only to be held in contempt, but to be held for two hours by the authorities – whose paranoia about security was, it turned out, the explanation for their actions. Only someone with malign intent, it was reasoned, could attend an Olympic event and not wear (to use Peter Cook's words about Harold Macmillan) a stupid great grin spread all over their silly face. I wonder if it was an unconscious suspicion that such an unwritten law was in effect that prompted my own patronizing effort when I attended the Women's Épée at the ExCel.

In an article in the same paper today is something which

at first looks only superficially related but is in fact more deeply so: a piece by Suzanne Moore, a columnist whom I often find acute, entertaining and provocative. The last of these qualities now manifested itself, as far as I am concerned, with a stance of almost aggressive affection for the whole Olympic spectacle. 'It's a wonderful combination of equal opportunity, ogling, admiration and, aaaw shucks, another medal! It's not just the taking part, it's the winning.' I do not want to turn this book into a spiral of counter-comment on various media commentators, but Moore's words are an important articulation of the pro-Olympics point of view, and so are worth engaging with.

Particularly worth noting is the disjunction between the sixth and seventh words of the first sentence, and the final one of its second, which strongly suggest that Moore's thoughts have not run round the track of her brain, but darted across the middle of it. This is, literally, a short circuit: an attempt to reclaim the event for the virtues of the left, a happy but wobbly conflation of the general racial, social and national inclusiveness of the whole event which at the same time sees no contradiction between this and the fundamental elitism of the very idea of a medal table. This is one narrative of the Games: a Benetton advert of an event, and a benign one, but one that does not recognize the great lists of defeats that are going on both within and without the Games' various arenas.

But this is more or less the official narrative, or the one that is most pleasing to the authorities. It would suit them, after all: this is happy hysteria for its own sake, and it is not risible that people with neither knowledge nor even the vaguest familiarity with certain sports are now screaming with delight when someone from their country does well: *it is the whole point.*

This year has seen something of a Quantitative Easing of good vibes: the injection of huge amounts of party atmosphere into the nation in order to improve a mood that might otherwise have turned ugly, what with the disappearance of half the summer and of all our money. The trouble is that, as is the case with QE, it is a short-term fix which may have damaging repercussions further down the line, leaving us far worse off than we were before. And the man arrested for not smiling is like someone receiving a billion-Reichsmark note with the purchasing power of a box of matches, and saying 'this is funny money'. The chilling thought I have is this: what would the consequences to Mr Worsfold have been if his unsmiling visage had not been the result of a congenital illness, but pure disapproval?

Meanwhile, in the freezing waters of the Serpentine (figuratively speaking; literally speaking, 14 degrees Celsius – not warm, especially if you're swimming 10 kilometres through it), the Brazilian competitor is pulled out of the water before her time, looking half-dead. Make no mistake, this is a brutally gruelling event. Our own best competitor, the 2009 and 2011 world champion Keri-Anne Payne (whose lithe polyurethane-clad form has been gracing the pages of colour supplements for what seems like years now; even I knew who she was before the Games started), is not in the lead, as we had been given to believe was her right. And why is this, we demand, outraged? There's your explanation right there:

David Cameron, in the crowd, jinxing Team GB. The race started at noon; by half-past one she is in 'the leading group' but not actually in the lead.

The swimmers reach the second 'feeding station', as if they were so many zoo animals. Each nationality's coach sticks out a bottle on the end of a pole with the relevant flag on it, the swimmers quickly roll onto their backs, drink as much as they can, toss the bottles into the water, and carry on, ploughing through the water, although the scale of the lake they're swimming in, and the height of the camera filming them, makes it look as though they are hardly moving at all: their task looks Sisyphean. (Although, at an average of almost exactly 5 km/h, their speed is that of a leisurely stroll through, say, the park that surrounds them.) Of all the sports I have seen so far, this looks like the one I would be least happy to participate in, were I to be forced to do so. It is held in real open water (known hitherto, to the majority of the public, as a swimming venue for various lunatics who thrash about in it on New Year's Day) instead of a chlorinated pool, with high-tech underwater cameras tracking the swimmers' motion. There is something raw about this event, *cru* as the French say, as in unpasteurized: it should carry a health warning.

At the fifth lap, out of six, Payne is in fifth place, and Cameron is not getting the message and leaving, so as to give her a chance while he still can ... and finally – swimmers have to reach up and slap a board with their hands to signal their completion of the race – Payne comes fourth, and the Curse of Cameron strikes again.

'Fourth in the world is not too bad,' she says graciously in her post-swim interview. Me, I'm amazed she can even speak at all, and is not being rushed off in an ambulance to the nearest cardiac unit.*

Later in the afternoon, I watch the BMX men's quarter-final. I had read reports of this sport with some scorn; it seemed to me like just one more factitious, crowd-pleasing addition to the roster, a kids' recreation, nodding towards an alternative, urban culture (albeit a slightly dated one), not, surely, a proper sport.

Still, it is extraordinary to watch, as eight riders (it seems like there are twice as many) hurl themselves round a wobbly, bouncy track, soaring into the air so often that you suspect the brief duration of each race is not so much to protect the riders, as to stop the audience from getting seasick. It is very, very dangerous, mind-bogglingly so even from

---

* Incidentally, two of the capital's major A&E units, at Charing Cross and Hammersmith hospitals, have been marked for closure by the government, thus leaving a very big hole in London's emergency provision. (West London's only A&E department will then be at St Mary's, Paddington, a hospital I was very strongly advised to avoid by a doctor friend of mine who had done his medical training there. Of course, that was some time ago, but it's the kind of advice that tends to stick in the mind.) A 'consultation' about this with provision for public attendance was arranged for the very day when half of West London's roads were to be closed off for the cycling, an amazing coincidence which meant that as few people as possible were able to attend without actually having to lock them in their own homes. As I write, the fate of the hospitals is uncertain, and even the local Tory MP, doubtless with a nervous eye on his majority, is giving his support to the protestors.

the safety of the living room, and at one point I see a pile-up of seven of the eight riders from which it seems only by a fluke that they're able to walk away unaided. There is also, I discover from someone who used to be a champion at this sport, an abnormally high rate – I mean *really, freakishly* abnormally high rate – of suicides and drug overdoses among its practitioners and ex-practitioners (the drug of choice being, I gather, crystal meth). This seems to be the most gladiatorial of the sports I have seen – perhaps because it recalls nothing so much as a horseless variant of the chariot race from *Ben Hur*.

Horsey dancing: at this late stage, the horseys are allowed to dance to music. (At first I thought I was watching highlights with some inspirational soundtrack overlaid.) The British team's opening choice: music from *The Lion King*, including the 'akuna matata' song, the one which says, basically, 'don't worry, be happy'. (This is a very different message, by the way, from *The Jungle Book*'s version of good-natured insouciance: in the earlier film, we were told that all we had to do was enjoy the 'bear necessities' – or, to look at it another way, forswear consumerism. The *Lion King* song says, instead, don't grumble. A small but telling difference, no?) I may add that making horses dance to a medley of the kind of mindlessly upbeat music you'd find piped into the nightclub toilets of a mid-scale holiday resort strikes me as one of the greatest cruelties that can be visited upon a noble and blameless animal, and if anyone tells me that the horses like it, I will give them a little lecture about the dangers of anthropomorphism,

the pathetic fallacy, and the dangers to civilization of debili-
tatingly bad taste. If I were a horsey in this event, I'd just
flatly refuse to move a muscle, except, perhaps, for an imperi-
ous twitch of the ear. Then I'd be shot.*

In an interview afterwards, one of the riders confesses
that the music is not her horse's 'favourite thing'.

* Although I have to confess a laugh escapes me when one of the British
team's choices proves to be the music from *The Great Escape*. The medley
continues, for the same horsey, with the fight music from the old James
Bond movies and 'Land of Hope and Glory', which brings out the whining leftie in me at his whiniest, and prompts a huge, exasperated, rolling
of the eyes.

10 August 2012

DAY 14

....

BMX
Triathlon
Netball
Synchronized Swimming

....

Preparing some lunch in the kitchen with the TV on in the living room, I am listening to a couple of cyclists being interviewed off-screen while the men have their go at churning their way round and round the Serpentine in the 10km Open Water. Well, not really listening ... more overhearing. I am beginning to reach a kind of saturation point with the Olympics, as I am fairly confident is the case even for those with a more casual interest in the Games than I have been obliged to take. It is all washing over me; everything is becoming a blur. I am wondering what else there is to say about it all, and I have just seen a BBC advertisement announcing, in eight days' time, the start of the new football season. An article in the *Daily Telegraph* by Richard Preston has contrasted the mind-bendingly rigorous training of the top Olympic athletes, as well as their generally modest and self-effacing manner, with the vastly overinflated wages and generally vile behaviour of Premiership footballers (who do rather less training). Although I suspect that the mood of the country is perhaps overestimating the saintliness of Olympic athletes, and that maybe not all footballers in the Premier League are appalling shits with the morals of alley cats, I suspect he's not far off the mark.

But then one of the cyclists being interviewed is asked about whether she would like to go on the popular television show *Strictly Come Dancing*. And although I can't recall the exact words, because I had a piece of toast in my hand and couldn't take notes, it will not be a distortion of the historical record to say that the reply went along the lines of 'I'd love to do *Strictly*. It's always been a dream.' She adds that the charity work she'll be doing, and further bike training, will take precedence, but still . . .

Meanwhile, a row is brewing about another aspect of the legacy: Boris Johnson, with fond memories of playing the Eton Wall Game presumably a large part of his mental make-up (he was a notoriously aggressive player, and according to his unofficial biography by Sonia Purnell, the school magazine composed the rhyme 'Hey, hey, ABJ, how many Oppidians did you kill today?'*), suggested that every school

---

* In English: 'Oppidian' is Eton's term for the typical Eton student, one whose parents can afford the massive fees for the school. Johnson was a scholar, that is, one whose academic ability meant his parents paid greatly reduced fees. The school being what it is, those who were clever enough

should now have two hours of compulsory PE a day. This has caused terror among my unathletic friends, and indeed me. Cameron has tried to defend his policy of axing compulsory PE by saying that it was because too many schools – or too many for him – were offering non-Olympic sports such as 'Indian dancing, or whatever' as an option. At which point, as if to show how easy Cameron's knack is for offering an open goal to his opponents – how delightfully luckless he is, what a tin ear he has, and how he can make those who were either ambivalent about, or even tentatively hostile to, a manifestation of popular culture-can make us suddenly aware that, actually, after all, we're not ambivalent or hostile any more – Nileeka Gunawardene, artistic director of Bollywood Dance London, suggested he try it himself. Cameron was 'challenged to', as ramped up by the press – in this case, the *Daily Telegraph*, in a spin on the less antagonistic words actually used which would have done the *Guardian* proud. That Cameron's reputation continues to tank as the Games unfold, even to their conclusion, is a massive gift to the nation, a sign of hope for future troubled times, and unless this is all part of a very cunning plan, in which he will emerge in the final straight as a winner, which

---

to get a discount on the education were scorned and patronized by those who had the money. This, together with Johnson's well-documented stinginess, casts an interesting light on an aspect of his ambition and concealed resentment that might help to remove the enigma from the man who was well described by Will Self as 'an enigma wrapped in a whoopee-cushion'. The 'ABJ' of the school refrain refers to the initials of Johnson's real name, although, for reasons of scansion, they missed out at the end the 'DP' of 'de Pfeffel'.

seems increasingly unlikely, we can see that the Tories are not going to benefit from these Games in the way some of us feared they would, and old-fashioned Olympian ideas about fair play, honour and common decency will not only triumph, but be seen to be antithetical to both the theory and practice of Tory ideology.

The *Daily Express* and the *Daily Mirror*, we learn, have big pictures of the Dutch dressage team proudly showing off their bronze medals; yet their captions insist that these are, instead, the British team showing off their golds. It is inconceivable that these venerable newspapers of record could have made a mistake, so there must be something wrong with my eyes instead.

'Having a well-earned silver medal celebratory cuddle' – this is what we've been doing for the last two weeks: giving ourselves a cuddle.

BMX – helmeted, visored, peaked – is the face of the future, the closest we have to Rollerball, the dystopian sport in which humanity was distracted from their condition by a stylized fight to the death. Crashes are not far off being the rule rather than the exception in BMX racing, as far as the coverage I have seen indicates; and indeed it falls naturally into that category of sports whose spectators watch ghoulishly in anticipation of violent mishap.

Even the commentators agree that the race is 'something of a lottery'. The only tactic, as far as I can see, is the blindingly obvious one to get in front and stay there, otherwise you are at risk of getting caught in a pile-up. (Which would seem to happen more in men's races than women's.)

Literalwatch: the commentator on Mariana Pajon, the Colombian BMX racer – 'her home town, Medellin will be on fire – not literally, I mean.' I gather that this commentator is actually more of a BMX expert than a professional media man – hence a self-correction which is by any measure a gross breach of broadcasting protocol, for which he will doubtless be ostracized.

I notice that the competitors in the triathlon (and I noticed this too in the open water yesterday, but at the time thought nothing of it) have their team affiliation and running number stencilled onto their bare arms. Something about this strikes me as an affront: the idea of the skin having a number on it has all sorts of uncomfortable associations. Well, two, really: the numbers tattooed onto the skin of Jews and other un-desirables incarcerated by the Nazis, prior to their immolation; and the branding of cattle. And yet, and yet . . . I am not quite sure how to put this, or even if I should put it in any way at all, but there is something . . . sexy about this. It suggests total dedication, as if the skin were itself nothing more than a uniform, or a tracksuit, something you put on in order to compete. And it draws attention to the musculature, in a way that tattoos now fail to do, because their ubiquity in modern life has rendered them almost invisible, the opposite of what they were meant to declare, an expression of individuality.

A top skateboarder/snowboarder is being interviewed explaining how the younger generation is more open to new sports, etc., etc. They show footage of him snowboarding as he talks; and then they cut to him. He has the mandatory flowing locks that one would expect of the snowboarder, but he is *wearing a bow tie*. For some reason I find this hugely engaging.

I have a chance to catch up with some men's netball. A sport which I had hitherto considered perhaps a little effete, historically for girls, turns out to be – at least when Russia and Bulgaria are playing – more brutal than rugby. Doubtless various received opinions are helping to form this impression, but I have to say the people playing this game don't just look like thugs. They look like *assassins*.

And finally, I get to see some synchronized swimming. This is an event which traditionally has always, without intending to, given rise to great hilarity. One remembers the French team who made a valiant stab at attempting an interpretation of the Holocaust; and a Japanese team courting international disbelief when they decided to have their own take on the Kobe earthquake. The British team do something based on *Peter Pan*, but I am too busy laughing to assess it respectfully. And it is an extraordinarily *silly* sport: the legs opening and closing like scissors, for example, a routine very familiar to me from so many Busby Berkeley films watched in childhood, on wet Sunday afternoons on the telly when there was nothing else to do ... well, what is all that about? The point is, our laughter at its absurdity is a much more forgiving and indulgent laughter than that which invariably accompanies the interpretative dances which take place on dry land, in subsidized theatrical space. That's more like scorn, a strong wish that one were somewhere else, licensed premises perhaps, and that all the performers were put into some sort of protective custody and taught to do something either more productive or less irritating. As it is, though the synchronized swimming is a scream, it is nevertheless a supremely engaging spectacle whose participants have obviously spent so long dreaming up and then practising their moves that you wonder how they ever found time to eat or sleep. There is also a kind of innocence to the sport, for all that it is about women's glistening legs, that makes us only roll our eyes when they try to re-create human evil or natural disaster, instead of calling for the sport's suppression. I'm not quite saying I could watch this all day – but I have to leave early to go to the Olympic Park, and I am finding it hard to tear myself away. I never thought I would write those last nine words. About synchronized swimming.

At last, for the first time, I go to the Olympic Park itself, as opposed to the more peripheral venues. Or rather, strictly speaking, the TV studios that have been set up by Channel 4 (and many others) at the top of the Westfield car park. The whole set-up is rather exciting: within the jerry-rigged marquee, strewn with bunting, are hundreds of flickering screens, the foot-soldiers of TV wandering around, it's like *M*A*S*H*. The sun hangs low and hot and heavy in the hazy sky, and the views – of the floodlit stadium, the absurd red tower like a tangled cable no one has the will to unravel, the Shard, perpetually shrouded, like a structure out of Tolkien, in its own malignity – seem unreal, a hallucination; or a dream that you struggle to make sense of on waking.

On the way back via St Pancras, I notice a couple of policemen carrying guns, not only holstered pistols, but fearsome-looking rifles. I scrutinize their faces. Their expressions are blankly watchful, unreadable, but we can read things into blank surfaces, especially when there is lethal weaponry involved. For a moment I feel real, boiling rage, on the point of bursting out into words. 'I just want you to know,' I feel like saying, 'that I don't like armed police in my town.' From having read Mike Thomas's novel *Police Notebook*, which is not a great work of art but a terrifying look inside the mind of a tactical firearms officer (written by someone who knows whereof he speaks), I am aware that this would be unwise. The contrast between these black-clad sinister psychopaths and the cheerful volunteers with their silly big foam hands could not be starker. Friends of mine have been deeply un-settled by the sight of soldiers in the streets of London – but the soldiers haven't been carrying guns.

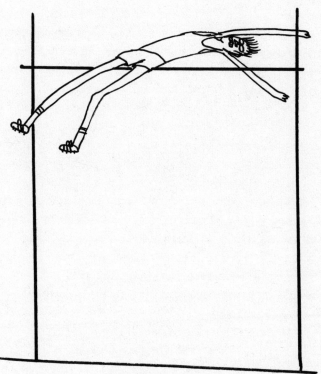

STUPID

11 August 2012

DAY 15

I wake, feeling as if my whole ENT system has been furred. It is either a cold, a reaction to the high pollen count or exhaustion – or a combination of two or all of these things. I am, I have to say, getting somewhat jaded with this enterprise, and feel that my willpower – never the most robust of my character traits – is flickering. The thought of writing somewhere around 2,000 words today, again, is extremely dispiriting. Few writers I know, and fewer of any note, leap into the writing chair in the morning, crack open the plastic piano and start pounding away with a song in their heart and a whistle on their lips; and I do so less than most I know. Feeling lousy on top of this just puts the tin hat on it. Despite the finishing line being in sight – or, more likely, precisely *because* it is in sight – I am beginning to feel more and more like Dorando Pietri, who on entering the stadium at the end of the 1908 Olympic marathon race in the lead was so bewildered and exhausted that he started running the wrong way and was helped to the line by two sympathetic officials (whose names – Jack Andrew and Dr Michael Bulger – live on, touchingly, to this day). He was disqualified, but Queen

Alexandra gave him a gilded silver cup the day after, which was very nice of her, don't you think?

I listen, as is my pleasure on weekends, to *Pick of the Pops* on Radio 2, a show I adore despite Tony Blackburn's delivery and flubs (this week he refers to the TV show starring George Cole and Dennis Waterman as 'The Minder', the mistaken definite article as painful an insertion as a jab in the face with a fork). Selections are played from the Top 30 of two more or less randomly chosen years. At the moment I have my epiphany, I am listening to a perhaps partial but still evocative choice of tunes from 1982 (Kid Creole and the Coconuts; Bananarama; 'Eye of the Tiger'). Not songs that featured in my collection, or ones I ever sought out, but familiar enough, even thirty years down the line, to be instantly recognizable. I catch myself wondering what the soundtrack will be for this summer, thirty years from now, and realize there will be none. The Olympics *are* the soundtrack, for pop music is no longer something that drifts through the air and floats into every home or room, through the keyholes and under the lintels like a benign, nationwide version of an old-fashioned London peasouper. The culture, if I may repeat such a now-hackneyed observation, is atomized, fragmented; we no longer all watch the same TV programmes; we fill up the social void of daily interaction and tweet and Facebook our news to people we have never met. So it is only natural that we fall so ardently on something that about half the people in the country have been following (that's quite a lot). Before the Games, there was a clear division, and some antagonism, between those who were looking forward to them and those who were not; now, voices against the Games are almost impossible to find. Anyway, the debate now is on wider terms. My own inner naysayer has been largely stifled or is dormant; and who can criticize what your consciousness gives you when you sleep? (The notion of the Olympics as a dream is something I am finding increasingly difficult to dismiss as a factitious and straw-grasping attempt to get some kind of intellectual traction on the spectacle: as I write these words, I am watching yet more showjumping, where the horses – those potent symbols of the unconscious, as Ted Hughes knew so well – jump, again, over fences whose posts are fake gas-lamps, miniature Stonehenges, pillar boxes.*)

★

* In the news today: Rob Smith, a Lymington restaurateur, has been arrested – *arrested*: held in a police cell overnight and released on bail – for spray-painting a Post Office box gold, in honour of the sailing champion Ben Ainslie, who lives in the town. (In a fun detail, CCTV footage confirms that he committed this terrible crime at 1.30 a.m., although in his defence this is a perfectly legitimate time for a bar and restaurant owner to be getting back from work.) The Royal Mail as it happens already had plans to repaint one of their pillar-boxes somewhere as yet unspecified in Cornwall – where Ainslie grew up. In a bid to show that they have a sense of humour about the whole business, and have caught the happy-go-lucky mood that has swept the nation, Royal Mail spokesman Heulyn Gwyn Davies said, 'We are extremely disappointed that someone has chosen to vandalize this particular post box. It is illegal to tamper with any of our post boxes and we are liaising with our engineers to ensure that it is repainted red as soon as possible.'

(Why 'this particular post box'? Could he have got away with it if he'd painted the one in Church Lane round the corner instead? Or gone a couple of miles down the road to Milford on Sea?)

Reluctant to follow the Games or even think about them much, I decide, if that is the right word to describe a non-decision, to arse about on Twitter, and note that Carol Ann Duffy's poem about the Games, printed on page 1 of today's *Guardian*, is trending; or rather, parodies of it are. It is, considered as a work of art, appalling, *bien-pensant* doggerel, all the more galling because my politics are, I would suspect, entirely in line with hers, and I whack off three or four parodies of my own ('We are poets, we are Carol/Scraping the bottom of the barrel', etc.), which are gratifyingly retweeted by many. I am not alone in thinking this way, you see. I then catch a tweet from the comedian Robert Webb, saying that he had unfollowed some 'journo' who had been snotty about her verse. I cannot pretend that this does not upset me deeply. I am proud, pathetically, of such well-known followers as I have, and to lose one like this feels uncomfortably close to being dumped. I respond as graciously as I can to this – in other words, not terribly graciously, but in as dignified a manner as Twitter allows: I announce that I have been unfollowed by Webb, but say that I still find him funny, 'so there'. At which point he in his turn replies graciously by refollowing me, and we have a brief but friendly conversation shaking hands and making up. Later on, reflecting on this bizarre little episode, in which poetry, the celebrity/non-celebrity divide and the way this is turning into a truly national conversation are all entangled, I realize that, for the time being at least, this country really has gone down the rabbit hole, and there is something wonderful about this; and precedented, for Britain has always had a natural gift for surrealism, however much it has often suited itself to pretend this is not the case.

I am aware, though, that there has been a (largely unnecessary) drive to whip up our emotions so that only the chilliest of heart, or the emotionally arid or autistic, can fail to be aroused; and it is this that makes me a bit suspicious. Decades of watching dystopian sci-fi films, *Invasion of the Body Snatchers* in particular, have trained me to be wary when everyone is in agreement. Not that a mass consensus is invariably a bad thing: I think that on the whole it was rather good, to put it mildly, that more or less everyone in the country was very keen on defeating Nazi Germany. (An example that will live in folk memory for some time to come still, however dismayed the Germans feel about this: wartime Britain an example of 'good' demagoguery, Hitler's Germany a very easily identifiable example of the bad kind.) But let's keep an eye on the techniques that are being used just in case we forget to sing from the same hymn sheet: the synthesis, for example, of well-worn songs with montages of sporting achievements a necessity (to the extent that some sports – dressage and beach volleyball, to take but two – actually now cannot take place without accompaniment) because that way it synthesizes its own immediate nostalgia. Which is one way of explaining why everyone has become so *emotional* about these Games: they are picking up the slack that pop music's departure from the collective consciousness has left.

Meanwhile, in the Pentathlon (or is it the Heptathlon? The Biathlon? The Dodecathlon? It is all becoming a blur) I am disappointed that when it comes to the shooty bit, the contestants fire laser pistols rather than ones which go bang, with bullets. I know I am prone to Luddism, and am on the alert to keep it in check, but this does seem an innovation too far.

An incredibly laboured joke about what would happen if Mo Farah (whose elevation to Hero status, and his defence of his loyalties, is to be greatly welcomed, and not only because the *Daily Mail*'s earlier denunciation of 'Plastic Brits', with him in mind, has left it with very smelly egg all over its face) were running on grass: they'd be saying 'Fly, Mo!' So although I wish him well in his upcoming race, I am going to watch *Dad's Army* on BBC2, the one where Hodges challenges the Home Guard to a cricket match, which I am sure will provide me with all sorts of reflections on the nature of competition and the nobility of sport.

Well, here's one reflection: the arcane rules of some sports (the *Dad's Army* episode, while respecting cricket's, makes much comic capital out of them) are the point; and the very straightforward rules of others also. In this sense, 'the Olympics' represent a totality: with some events involving rules which are either obscure or, to the layman, utterly unquantifiable – e.g. synchronized swimming – what we are cheering on is the abstract idea of 'sport' itself. As it is, I note from casual glances at Twitter, that Farah has excelled himself and delighted a nation, and that my deliberate absence from this event makes me feel as though I have missed out, as if on a really good party; my consolation being only the title of this book, which implied that part of my brief is to make a point of not getting involved from time to time. And although fatigue has been setting in – not just because of the writing but because of the passive watching – for the first time I find myself thinking of Shakespeare's lines about gentlemen in England now a-bed, kicking themselves for not having been around for a moment of glory. The comparison between bloody battle and a few gruelling laps round a track which one is only watching on TV anyway makes this sound ridiculous, I know, but as Huizinga has pointed out, these contests are a substitute for more lethal ones, and create the same kind of emotions in both spectators and protagonists, but without the loss of life. But there you go: I missed Mo. I feel I've let my publisher down, I've let my agent down, I've let my friends and family and girlfriend down, I've let the cat down, but most of all I've let myself down.

Gold for Ed McKeever in the kayaking – in humbled reference to my previous remarks about kayaking on Day 6, his performance – and those of all the others – in the final of the Kayak single 200m sprint makes me realize that there is more to this sport than I had imagined. In fact, the way they barrel along in a perfect straight line, at great speed, using what would be for me the wayward movements of the arms, makes a great impression, something almost chilling about it in the way that the vagaries of the body have been marshalled to produce something mathematical in its precision. It is both human and inhuman, and a kind of awe is the only possible fully human response. (That McKeever is, in real life, or waking life, a trainee accountant only adds to this, although I fear that kayaking's gain will be accountancy's loss.)

★

The time has come for Tom Daley not only to win himself a medal and redeem his failure of a few days earlier, but to help us in our reclamation of interest in the whole spectacle, which is now, even to a sympathetic eye, beginning to accrete the atmosphere of a party that has been going on maybe a bit too long: people are becoming sloppy, either getting into fights or tearfully embracing each other, vowing eternal friendship. Mo Farah jolted everyone back into delight, but that was a race, something where anyone can grasp the way the result is determined. With diving, we are on shakier ground, and have to rely on the judges, however much we flatter ourselves we have begun to understand the fine details between a merely very good dive and an excellent one. We are back, then, in the arena of abstract sport, where all we know, if we are to be honest with ourselves, is whether someone has won or lost, and not *how* someone has won or lost. We are in the hands of experts; yet who, here, in this context, dares complain about elitism? No one can say, 'I don't know much about diving, but I know what I like,' and claim with a straight face that this is a perfectly valid response. But at least this nice young man, every parent's ideal son, about whom it is now, without exaggeration, illegal to say anything mean, does well, and the country sighs in pleasure and relief, his bronze medal atoning for his earlier disgrace, and being treated pretty much as if he had won a gold.

DAY 16

....

Men's Marathon
Mountain Biking
Handball
Rhythmic Gymnastics
Closing Ceremony

....

Yesterday, the daily bulletin from Transport for London about travel disruptions to the Games warns me of tomorrow's marathon, so I decide not to go for my daily 26-mile run through the streets of leafy West London, and confine myself to nipping over the road and replacing the milk which had curdled in my morning tea despite having four days left on its clock. I am minded to make a scene, but such is the mood of the country, a feeling of benevolence and public spirit, that I do not, and I resist the temptation to insert a metaphor about either my mood, or that of the country, itself curdling. The country's certainly has not: but there is an air of melancholy to the hysteria, as on the last full day of a holiday. Although mentally packing up, there is still a determination to wring the last gouts of pleasure from the spectacle, and for some reason there is a fitting reification of this feeling when watching both the marathon and the mountain biking.

The marathon does not appear to be as gruelling as it used to be in the days of Dorando Pietri, for the leader, Uganda's Stephen Kripotich, is not only insouciant enough to collect a Ugandan flag from a spectator during the last stages of the race, he looks, as he breasts the tape, so in command of his breath that he could, were he told to, turn round and run the whole course again. And to think that when I have to run up the twenty-odd stairs at Shepherd's Bush Market station to catch a train, I collapse into the carriage worried that I will drop down dead, gasping from exhaustion, and give all the other passengers a fright.

The mountain biking looks more gruelling, as the cyclists toil up and down the hills and paths of Hadleigh Farm in Essex. This is the most Sisyphean of sports: as they reach the top of the incline, in the lowest gear possible, they seem to be almost stationary, even though their legs are going round; much as (the scientists tell us) an astronaut at the event horizon of a black hole, though about to be consumed and torn to a string of atoms by gravity in an instant, will appear to the distant observer, thanks to the effects of time dilation and relativity, virtually motionless, suspended in eternity, on the brink of nowhere, but going nowhere.

And the progress of the cyclists seems stately, not as if they're competing against each other, but simply going for a ride together, the two leaders, the Czech Kulhavy and the Swiss Schurter, ahead of the pack by some distance but travelling along companionably. Then, towards the end of the race, they start overtaking each other, and a proper contest looks on the cards. I start pumping a sympathetic leg again, as I did with Wiggins, even though I have no interest in who wins (although my distant roots in central Europe incline me towards the Czech; but I do not really feel this at the time; as far as I am concerned, they're both the underdogs, and I just want to see a good, clean, noble contest. What the hell, I ask myself later, has happened to me?). For some reason I am curiously affected by the old-fashioned bell which is rung to announce the final lap. Perhaps, it occurs to me later, because it recalls the bell rung in pubs for last orders: time, gentlemen, please.

The men's super heavyweight boxing final, and Anthony Joshua wins the gold, and – another confounding of the notion that you have to train from the womb in order to succeed – only four years after stepping into a boxing ring for the first time in his life. He, like Chris Hoy, has a face it is impossible to dislike; in fact, he is almost too handsome. But then he sticks his medal in his mouth – it is a rather more puzzling gesture than the now-traditional bite. He looks strangely foolish, innocent, as if by a trick of scale he has turned into a child and is sucking on a big gold lollipop, or a chocolate whose foil he is not yet dextrous enough to unwrap. Has he, in his mind, reverted to infancy, when babies find out about the things of the world not so much by handling or looking at them, but by putting them in their mouths?

I check out the final of the men's handball. This is, as far as I can see, an excuse for a mass punch-up. In abstract I am fond of the Swedes, whose reputation for pacific behaviour is largely an earned one, but this bunch are just crazed with violence. There is a wild look in their eyes, as if they have gone beyond the limits of human morality, and I suddenly can imagine, vividly, the terror which would have been felt by the villagers on a Yorkshire coast in the tenth century as the longboats appeared over the horizon. At one point it looks as though one of them actually nuts a French player, at which juncture, finally, a foul is declared.

There is a French player called Narcisse, or Narcissus. Who will not keep his looks if he plays against the Swedes again. They are, though, defeated narrowly; after the match, the madness will leave them, and they will suddenly become progressively social democrat, and work hard towards the rehabilitation of offenders.

Finally, I get to catch up with the rhythmic gymnastics. This is the routine with the twirly ribbons and the hula-hoops. To the sound of the *William Tell* overture (unidentified by the commentator except as 'stirring' until the famous bit kicked in) the Italian team, a Berlusconi fantasy of smiling girls in leotards with pulled-back hair, cavort around the stage, hurling and catching their hula-hoops with tightly choreographed precision. But they are not as tightly choreographed as the Russians who went before them, who were so disciplined they managed to get their ribbons to twirl *with exactly the same shapes*, the same configurations of flow. This is again preposterous as sport, but undeniably involving as spectacle.

With this routine, the realization smacks me between the

eyes that what this Olympics has been about really is *circus*: a circus drained of animal cruelty (although it still has its horses, endless jumping horses: there's been the women's pentathlon earlier today, with less specialist riders, on horseys from a horsey pool of horseys for hire, knocking off more poles from the jumps than I have seen beforehand), and with the ancient Roman element of sacrifice and murder replaced by the rituals of victory on the podium and weeping losers. (Weeping winners, too, of course.)

Duty compels me to watch the final, running, bit of the women's modern pentathlon; it is, after all, the last event, and we are in with a chance. And ... well, you know the result. The Lithuanian (at the time of writing, the BBC website records the fact that Samantha Murray has won silver, but it does not record the gold medallist's name*) Laura Asadauskaite, wins, and her smile as she breaks the tape is so engaging that I instantly fall a little bit in love with her, and want to do something so special for her that I will get to see that smile again. She even – and this is a bit I *really* like – pauses before she hits the tape, and holds it in her hands, as if it is a silk scarf someone has given her for Christmas, and she wants to admire it before putting it round her neck.

Here is a foretaste of what is to come: a disappointing photograph of Mo Farah doing his 'Mobot' signature gesture

---

* Even the next day, I have to look long and hard on the BBC website to find it out. This is a bit disgraceful, no?

alongside Cameron. I try and imagine an athlete saying, 'No, I won't stand next to him. I might consider standing next to Ed Miliband, though.' Could it ever happen?

And now the closing ceremony. I had personally witnessed what was either a change in the national mood or a localized deviation from it at about a quarter to eight on a sunny evening by Tower Bridge. The last day. A fat old chancer – a decrepit Del Boy type, a harmless extra in a modern Dickens skit – wearing a comedy Union Jack top hat was standing by his barrow, ranged with cheap tourist tat: clear plastic Big Ben paperweights, phone box and black cab money-boxes, you know the drill (the kind of stuff that Londoners actually tune out of their vision). But standing round him were three unsmiling City of London police officers, telling him to move on. Apparently, someone from within the Tower of London had seen his unauthorized pitch and told the police he had an injunction preventing him from being there; the trader said he had no such thing, and every right to be there.

I dawdled by the side of the road, using the traffic as an excuse to overhear what was going on. (I am always drawn to situations like this.) The WPC in the group came up to me and asked what I was doing. Waiting for a gap in the traffic, I replied. And, I admitted, picking up a little snapshot of London life. She asked me, unsmilingly, to move on. I gestured at the stream of cars. Her mood was turning ugly: this was no smiling bobby on the beat, but an impatient, overworked jack-in-office who was using her uniform not as a representative of the benign British state's concern for its citizens' welfare, but as a combined shield and weapon against it. I thought of my uniformed toy Wenlock (or Man-deville?) that stands on top of the fridge, his expression ambivalent, mutable even; at first I had assumed he looked reasonably cheery, but one night he was left out in the rain and since then he has been staring at us with a stern and pitiless gaze.

Sure, this fat old git with his barrowload of crap, hoping to make a few bob from the combined poor taste and good-will of people who couldn't know any better, wasn't exactly an adornment to the area; but he wasn't that out of place either, and all that stopped him from being there, and joining other vendors of crap, was his lack of a licence. And mean-while the Old Bill's good manners, strained by the effort of two weeks of smiling and helping bewildered Ecuadorians get from A to B, were beginning to unravel. The police, as you know, always turn up, in a bad mood, *en masse*, when a party starts getting too loud or going on too long.

Which has what to do with the closing ceremony? A lot, as it happened. As in the way Dorothy translates familiar elements of Kansas into outlandish ones in the land of Oz, so the ceremony was like a bad-dream version of the old git's barrow: the laziest tourist tropes about ahld Landan Tahn, tarted up; all giving the area a bad name – but in this case, the wretched spectacle had all the correct documentation, and no one in authority asked it to move on.

'Critics applaud Olympic closing ceremony' ran the head-line on the BBC website on 14 August 2012, but that wasn't the way the people saw it: a four-out-of-five star review by the *Guardian*'s theatre critic, Michael Billington, not only abdicated its own responsibility ('You can't really review a show like this. You can only describe it'), it was humiliated underneath from the very first comment below the line: 'Three words: it was shit.' I usually take the offensive comments left by pseudonymous readers as seriously as I would the scrawls on the wall of a pub jakes, but, overwhelmingly, that was the sentiment that kept being expressed. Just as the opening ceremony had united the nation, the closing ceremony did: against it. Billington was not alone, though.

The interesting thing was that those press commentators who had fallen quickly into line with the public mood once it became clear the Games were going to be a hit found themselves too slow-moving to realize that assent to the spectacle does not, thankfully, mean blind, unconditional and permanent adoration; or perhaps they were simply terrified of saying anything negative. The public, though, are under no such constraints, it seems, and in a way I found the reaction to the shambles ('a cacophony of British music' was how one *preview* described the forthcoming show, and the rest of the piece made it quite clear that the writer did not know the etymological derivation of the word 'cacophony'. It is 'shit sound') as heartening as any other of the public's reactions.

Actually, to say that the closing ceremony was like the bad dream of the vendor's barrow is to grant it rather too much intentionality. We were in the same kind of space, but from the moment that we had Timothy Spall as Churchill, poking his head out of Big Ben and declaiming the same speech by Caliban that Branagh as Brunel did in the opening ceremony, it was clear that what we were going to get from here on in was simply an uninspired knock-off of the original, a sort of fan-fiction version of it, only without that genre's legitimacy. If Boyle's show was best described and made sense of as a dream, one each of us seemed to experience in our own mind, then this was like listening, while the mind screamed for escape, to the very tedious dream of a very tedious person at a party whose best moments have now passed. And worst of all, when compelled to pay attention to the details, you suspected that this wasn't even a dream at all; it was all made up, an attempt by the bore in front of you to convince himself and everyone else that he does, in fact, remember his dreams, when in truth he does no such thing.

This was why it was all so hackneyed (and the taxis – hackneys, as they were once called – that the Spice Girls sang on top of were probably the only time that a metaphor was enacted; but not, I suspect, deliberately. The rest of it – Fatboy Slim inside a giant inflatable octopus, Annie Lennox in a gothic Viking longboat – was all image salad, an off-the-top-of-the-head rather than the from-the-recesses-of-the-mind trick that Boyle pulled off), the music the record collection of the unimaginative. Even the parts that were good were spoiled: Ray Davies telling us where the 'sha-la-las' were in 'Waterloo Sunset' ('at least McCartney didn't tell us when the "na na nas" in "Hey Jude" were coming up,' wrote a disgruntled Tweeter); George Michael boring a globe with an unwanted rendition of his new single; Eric Idle; Boris Johnson dancing like a fat fuck (for the very good reason that he is one); the surviving members of the Who, who unlike Keith Moon and Robert Entwistle have failed to die before they got old, singing 'My Generation' . . . And which would be worse? If there were deliberate design, or not, in having Jessie J singing the song 'Price Tag' (sample lyrics: 'it's not about the money . . . you can keep the cars') while being driven slowly around in a Rolls-Royce Phantom Drophead Coupé, price tag £305,000? (On another note, though, one wonders what people made of John Lennon's lines asking us to imagine 'no countries' in a stadium where the flags of 204 of them were blowing, and how many around the world were outraged that we were being exhorted to imagine no religion, too, as if imagining no countries wasn't bad enough. Again: fifth-form irony or brainless blunder? You decide.) As for hearing the opening notes of 'I Am the Walrus' but then discovering that it was going to be sung by Russell Brand . . . anyone care to venture why, save to vex us and dishonour the memory of a great song?

The most common response – and we have to take common responses into account when it comes to populist entertainment, especially when the responses chime with mine – was a roar of outrage and contempt (for a moment I confused the Who's 'Baba O'Riley' with 'Won't Get Fooled Again', a mistake surely the reaction of a disgusted preconscious), a complete contrast to what people had been saying and thinking for the rest of the Games, and that this was what the more alarmist among us had feared the opening ceremony was going to be like: a witless display of mediocrity, impoverished in every sense except the financial one. Proud to accept only Visa, indeed.

Boyle's vision was shored up by intellectual foundations. Frank Cottrell Boyce, his writer, had given him a copy of Humphrey Jennings's *Pandaemonium* before they started work: this is the collection, by the visionary (and surrealist-influenced) film-maker whose most popular achievements were the wartime films *Britain Can Take It, Fires Were Started* and *A Diary for Timothy* (this last, with an incredibly moving narration written by E. M. Forster addressed to a new-born child during a time of war, but with the hope for a new future, may even have triggered the idea of the giant baby being delivered in the ceremony, and the paean to the NHS). It's a work that brings together the contemporary responses – bewildered, amazed, shocked, astonished, delighted – of writers and diarists to the new technological achievements of the Industrial Revolution. Its influence on the ceremony is unmistakable; the very opening scene is called 'Pandaemonium'.*

---

* 'Pandaemonium' means 'all the demons'. It is the name Milton gives to the capital of Hell in *Paradise Lost*, and when you consider the hill in the opening ceremony, it's hard not to think of these lines (or rather, for me, once I'd been reminded of these lines after the event, the connection became obvious):

> There stood a Hill not far whose griesly top
> Belch'd fire and rowling smoak; the rest entire
> Shon with a glossie scurff, undoubted sign
> That in his womb was hid metallic Ore,
> The work of Sulphur. Thither wing'd with speed
> A numerous Brigad hasten'd. As when bands
> Of Pioners with Spade and Pickaxe arm'd
> Forerun the Royal Camp, to trench a Field,
> Or cast a Rampart. Mammon led them on,
> Mammon, the least erected Spirit that fell
> From heav'n, for ev'n in heaven his looks and thoughts
> Were always downward bent, admiring more
> The riches of Heav'ns pavement, trod'n Gold . . .

It is safe to say that Kim Gavin, the onlie begetter (so far as I know) of the closing ceremony, whose experience beforehand has been confined to staging concerts for Take That and Victoria Wood, has not read *Pandaemonium*, or seen any of Jennings's work. His choice as director was, then, impeccably populist – if by 'populist' you mean that subset of the creative industries that refuses to believe the ordinary public have it in them to be moved to wonder, or new worlds of thought. I am left to ponder whether it was deliberate, a very cunning ploy by Boyle to discredit a potential rival, or to make us all realize that we have woken up now, the dream has passed, and we are back in a very ordinary world, with our ordinary stories, our mediocre talents, our boring, unvivid, dead and dying dreams. The dream of a barrowman who imagined, for a while, that he was showcasing the best of a nation. Move along now. Everyone move along. Nothing to see here. Not any more.

Acknowledgements

Thanks first to Simon Winder, whose idea this was; to Derek Johns, my agent, to Hannah Griffiths, for all sorts of reasons, to Laurie Penny, who put up with me, and Toby Poynder, who provided, as always, expert emergency technical support when it was most needed.